James Hamblin Smith

Exercises on the elementary Principals of Latin prose Composition

With examination Papers on the elementary Facts of Latin Accidence and Syntax

James Hamblin Smith

Exercises on the elementary Principals of Latin prose Composition
With examination Papers on the elementary Facts of Latin Accidence and Syntax

ISBN/EAN: 9783337077440

Printed in Europe, USA, Canada, Australia, Japan

Cover: Foto ©ninafisch / pixelio.de

More available books at **www.hansebooks.com**

EXERCISES

ELEMENTARY PRINCIPLES OF

LATIN PROSE COMPOSITION

WITH

EXAMINATION PAPERS ON THE ELEMENTARY
FACTS OF LATIN ACCIDENCE AND SYNTAX

BY

J. HAMBLIN SMITH, M.A.

OF GONVILLE AND CAIUS COLLEGE, AND LATE LECTURER IN CLASSICS
AT ST. PETER'S COLLEGE, CAMBRIDGE

WATERLOO PLACE, LONDON
Oxford and Cambridge
MDCCCLXXVIII

PREFACE.

My chief object in writing this Book has been to construct a graduated series of English sentences capable of being turned into *rhythmical* Latin Prose.

Harmony in the arrangement of words in a sentence, is a mark of good Latin writing of no less value than purity of language, correctness of construction, or elegance of phrase.

The Exercises have been arranged so as to suit the order of the sections in my *Latin Grammar*, and the Latin equivalents for the words in each Exercise will generally be found in the Vocabularies given in the *Grammar*. Still, as I have given a complete English-Latin Vocabulary at the end of this book, it may be used with any elementary treatise on Latin Grammar.

The student should always have at hand a Latin-English Dictionary, that he may examine the various meanings of the words to which his attention is directed in the headings of the Exercises. Thus he will be led to observe that such words as *res, ago, duco*, have many

English equivalents, and to mark the difference of meaning in cognate words, as *animus* and *anima*, and in synonyms, as *peto, quaero, rogo*, and the like.

The Examination Papers have been constructed in imitation of the form in which similar questions are proposed in the *Previous Examination* at Cambridge. The concluding part of each of these Papers contains references to common differences of idiom in English and Latin.

I have only to add that I shall be grateful to any teacher who will give this little book a trial, and who will inform me of any errors, whether in the plan or in the performance of the work, that he may detect.

J. HAMBLIN SMITH.

42 TRUMPINGTON STREET,
    CAMBRIDGE, *March* 1878.

TABLE OF CONTENTS.

PAGE

EXERCISES IN LATIN PROSE COMPOSITION.

PART I

EXERCISE I.

ON THE INFLEXIONS OF VERBS.

Explained in the Grammar, § 15 to 22.

1. I was falling.
2. We shall sing.
3. Thou art sleeping.
4. He will come.
5. Ye will see.
6. I shall remain.
7. Wait.
8. We laugh.
9. We shall stand.
10. She was singing.
11. We are preparing.
12. He was ploughing.
13. She will rise.
14. Learn.
15. They were standing.
16. He will teach.
17. They will remain.
18. We were sleeping.
19. Write.
20. They are coming.

EXERCISE II.

SUBJECT AND VERB. § 15 to 32.

1. The boys will sing.
2. The boar was sleeping.
3. The poplar is green.
4. The eagle was flying.
5. The guests were sitting.
6. The trumpets are sounding.
7. The leaves were falling.
8. The girl will laugh.
9. The envoys will come.
10. The winds were rising.
11. The boys are writing.
12. The constellation is rising.
13. The master was standing.
14. The poet was writing.
15. The roses will fall.
16. The slave was waiting.
17. The door was open.
18. The handmaids will hear.
19. The drops were falling.
20. The guests will remain.

EXERCISE III.

THE ACCUSATIVE CASE. § 33.

NOTE.—*Words, in this and the following Exercises, printed in italics, are not to be rendered in Latin.*

Look out in your Latin-English Dictionary—peto, quaero ; littera, epistola; pateo, aperio.

1. The master was teaching the boys.
2. The slaves are adorning the tables.
3. We seek the shade.
4. The boys love *their* master.
5. The charioteer was driving *his* horses.
6. The wolf will frighten the lamb.
7. The girls were gathering apples.
8. We shall seek assistance.
9. The master will admonish the boys.
10. We shall see the moon.
11. We were afraid of Lepidus.
12. Fortune directs *our* life.
13. The boy is opening *his* eyes.
14. Pompeius will send a slave.
15. I was looking for you.
16. The sailor was carrying an oar.
17. Pompeius will send a letter.
18. God preserves the universe.
19. The elms will furnish shade.
20. I was writing a letter.

EXERCISE IV.

THE DATIVE CASE. § 34.

Look out pateo, aperio ; venia ; trado ; insidiae ; cena.

1. I will give you the book.
2. Give me the book.
3. The way will be open for us.

4. I will prepare the couch for you.
5. The inhabitants will hand over the town to us.
6. The plane affords shade to the calves.
7. The master will give me a reward.
8. The slaves will open the gate for *their* lord.
9. We will give gifts to the sailors.
10. They were preparing an ambuscade for Pompeius.
11. I will send you the letter.
12. The girl will gather a rose for you.
13. Pluck me an apple.
14. Open the door for me.
15. Prepare *my* dinner for me.
16. Give me *some* money.
17. The poet will tell us a story.
18. Grant me forgiveness.
19. Give me help.
20. Deliver up the sword to me.

EXERCISE V.

THE GENITIVE CASE. § 35.

Look out arma, telum ; seco, tondeo ; exemplum ; obtineo : castrum.

1. We praise the justice of Brutus.
2. We see the coast of Italy.
3. The weapons of fortune alarm me.
4. Hear *thou* the commands of the queen.
5. We are seeking the favour of Pompeius.
6. We fear the fortune of war.
7. We will cut the boughs of the poplar.
8. The leaves of the roses will fall.
9. We will open the gates of the town.
10. We shall see the camp of Labienus.
11. The boys were dreading the anger of *their* master.
12. The slave was cutting *his* lord's beard.
13. The girl was holding the boy's right hand.

14. We are looking for the son of Tarquinius.
15. The leaves of the elms will furnish us *with* shade.
16. I will send you a copy of the letter.
17. Send me a copy of the letter of Pompeius.
18. Clodius was seeking the favour of the people.
19. Despise the riches of Croesus.
20. We are in possession of the banks of the Rhine.

EXAMINATION PAPER A.

On § 1-35.

1. What letters are called Labials?

2. Write in full the Future Imperfect tenses of the verbs sēdāre, *to quench*, mŏvēre, *to move*, solvĕre, *to loose*, frangĕre, *to break*, ăgĕre, *to render, to perform*, sūmĕre, *to take*.

3. What are the Past Imperfect tenses of āvertĕre, *to put aside*, accēdĕre, *to approach*, augēre, *to increase, to enrich*, dōnāre, *to present*?

4. What are the Future Imperfect tenses of crescĕre, *to increase*, gĕrĕre, *to carry on*, nĕcāre, *to kill*, bibĕre, *to drink*?

5. Decline tuba, tenebrae, equus, ingenium, socer, locus, filia, fābŭla, *a play*, vĕnia, *excuse*, signum, *signal*, consilium, *counsel, advice, plan, design*.

6. What is the simplest use of the Dative case?

7. Render in Latin the following phrases :—

ENGLISH.	LATIN.
(1) to pitch a camp.	to place a camp.
(2) to break up a camp.	to move a camp.
(3) to make a signal.	to give a signal.
(4) to thank.	to render thanks.
(5) to exhibit a play.	to give a play.
(6) to act a play.	to perform a play.
(7) to punish.	to take penalties.
(8) to be punished.	to give penalties.
(9) to wage war.	to carry on war.
(10) to ask forgiveness.	to seek excuse.
(11) to poison.	to kill with poison.
(12) to make arrangements for.	to prepare.
(13) a signal for battle.	a signal of battle.
(14) forgiveness for a fault.	excuse of a fault.

EXERCISE VI.

THE ABLATIVE AND VOCATIVE CASES. § 36, 37.

Look out animus, anima; signum; dono; argentum; augeo; duco; necare veneno, dare venenum.

1. We will adorn the altar with boughs.
2. We soothe the troubles of the soul by sleep.
3. Labienus gives the signal with the trumpet.
4. Alexander will cut the knot with *his* sword.
5. I will pacify the anger of the queen with words.
6. The inhabitants were fortifying the town with a wall.
7. The boy was cutting an apple with *his* knife.
8. The farmer is drawing furrows with *his* plough.
9. The master will commend you, boys.
10. We fear thee, Crassus.
11. Go, *my* lad, get dinner ready.
12. Pamphilus, I am calling you.
13. Ask for help, Pompeius.
14. Arise, Valerius.
15. Govern *your* temper, boy.
16. Help me, Atticus, with *your* advice.
17. He will poison *his* father-in-law.
18. I will present you, Julia, with a ring.
19. The gods enrich me with wealth.
20. Slaves, deck the tables with plate.

EXERCISE VII.

PREPOSITIONS AND LOCATIVE CASE. § 38 to 40.

Look out voco; ago, duco, traho; gero; specto; porto, veho.

1. The leaves are falling in the woods.
2. We shall come from the shores of Italy.
3. I see thee in *my* dreams.
4. You will see me at Athens.
5. You seek advice from me.
6. The boy is rising from *his* bed.

7. The girl is sleeping on the couch.
8. I will invite you to dinner.
9. The messenger was coming to the queen.
10. We will drive the calves into the shade.
11. I will send envoys to the camp of Pompeius.
12. The smoke was rising from the altar.
13. The boy will remain at home.
14. Epaminondas was waging war in the Peloponnesus.
15. The Sicilians are seeking aid from us.
16. We shall be spectators of the games at Corinth.
17. *There* was at Delphi a statue of Lysander.
18. We are sending envoys to Corinth.
19. The slave of Tarquinius was carrying a letter to Gabii.
20. We will send envoys to Italy.
21. The girl was asleep under the plane-tree.
22. An adder is lying under the elm.
23. The master is conducting the boys through the wood.
24. The calves were lying on the ground.

EXERCISE VIII.

ADJECTIVES WITH STEMS IN *A* AND *O*. § 41 to 46.

Look out negotium ; ago ; foveo ; pecunia, nummus ; albus, candidus.

1. The lilies are white.
2. The poplars are tall.
3. The bank is steep.
4. The boys are good.
5. The plough was bent.
6. The woods were thick.
7. The boy has yellow hair.
8. We drink cold water.
9. We are learning new words.
10. The eggs are small.
11. You have active slaves.
12. The ass is lazy.
13. The business is important.
14. We have in hand an important matter.
15. We are waging a fresh war.
16. He has a large number of slaves.
17. Be kind to the sick girl.
18. I will give you a large *sum of* money.
19. He used to give many sums-of-money to *his* friends.
20. Good *men* have many friends.

EXERCISE IX.

I-NOUNS AND ADJECTIVES. § 47 to 54.

Look out integer, bonus; aedes, templum; fortuna; paro; consilium;
solvo, navis; amnis, rivus, fluvius.

1. We see the enemy's fleet.
2. The dog was watching the sheep.
3. A snake lies in the grass.
4. We seek shade in the valleys.
5. The sailors will prepare a raft.
6. The barren fields will become green.
7. The war will be advantageous.
8. We have an honest witness.
9. I will lead you to the doors of the temple.
10. The girl has a faithful dog.
11. The rivers fall into the sea.
12. The moon was rising from the clouds.
13. The cat loves *her* young.
14. Wretched is the condition of the citizens.
15. Clodius is arranging for a slaughter of honest *men.*
16. I will give you wholesome advice (*pl.*).
17. I am a Roman citizen.
18. The Gauls were fortifying the town with towers.
19. A stream was flowing through the vale.
20. The Romans were weighing anchor (*Lat.*, loose the ships).

EXERCISE X.

I-NOUNS AND ADJECTIVES—*continued.* § 47 to 54.

Look out laudo; praebeo; porta, ianua.

1. The birds were singing in the grove.
2. We will deck the sterns of the ships with garlands.
3. The fishes will come into the nets.

4. We shall laugh at the enemy's threats.
5. The enemy were breaking up *their* camp.
6. The master speaks highly of the boy's disposition.
7. We will chase the fox from the wood.
8. Gaul contains great abundance of iron.
9. The sheep will supply the farmer with wool.
10. We will quench *our* thirst with cold water.
11. Great was the slaughter *on the side* of the enemy.
12. Hand over to us the keys of the gates.
13. The situation is healthy.
14. We shall avoid the perils of the sea.
15. We have a kind father.
16. We shall see the girl's mother.
17. Mother, you are cruel.
18. I will conduct you, brother.
19. Father, I will wait for you at home.
20. Pompeius was leading his troops *down* to the sea.

EXERCISE XI.—Recapitulatory.

1. We are citizens of Rome.
2. I will stay at home.
3. He asks forgiveness for his fault.
4. I shall see you at Corinth.
5. We will seek advice from Crassus.
6. I thank you, Lentulus.
7. The girls are sitting under the elm.
8. I will gather you some roses.
9. The Germans are making preparations for war.
10. We shall fight in the shade.
11. The banks of the stream will be green with moss.
12. You will avoid the perils of the sea.
13. The Germans are breaking up *their* camp.
14. The boys are learning new words.
15. I will send a slave to Gabii.

16. The Helvetii will seek aid from us.
17. I invite you to dinner.
18. I will send you a copy of Cinna's letter.
19. The Germans are waging war in Gaul.
20. I receive gloomy letters from Clodius (use *mitto*).

EXAMINATION PAPER B.

On § 1-59.

1. Write in full the Future Imperfect tenses of ambulāre, *to walk*, ostendĕre, *to show*, făcĕre, *to make*, căpĕre, *to take*, vŏvēre, *to row*, mūtāre, *to change*, lŏcāre, *to station*, expōnĕre, *to explain*, irruĕre, *to rush in*, quaerĕre, *to search after*, trăhĕre, *to drag.*

2. Decline ignis, sitis, rete, mater, silvester, celer, honos, *a public office*, auctŏritas, *authority.*

3. Decline vilis, pes, laus, mas, mos, mus, seges, bos, ăcūtus, *sharp*, prātum, *meadow*, vŏluntas, *goodwill.*

4. What are the Genders and meanings of rus, mos, lapis, palus, silex, vos, arbor, oratio, pons, dolor, caput?

5. What is the common rule for the appearance or absence of *i* in the Genitive Plural? Mention exceptions.

6. Render in Latin the following phrases :—

ENGLISH.	LATIN.
(1) to deliver a speech.	to hold an oration.
(2) to pass *one's* life.	to perform life.
(3) to pass the night.	
(4) to seek renown.	to search after fame.
(5) to set an example.	to give an example.
(6) to build a bridge.	to make a bridge.
(7) to authorise.	to give authority.
(8) to be authorised.	to have authority.
(9) to sue for peace.	to seek peace.
(10) to be a candidate for office.	to seek a public office.
(11) a pain in the head.	a pain of the head.

EXERCISE XII.

CONSONANT-NOUNS. § 55 to 57.

Look out pratum, ager ; sol ; inventor ; traho ; praedo, latro ; mors, nex.

1. I will be your leader.
2. Give me *some* nuts.
3. We shall see light in the darkness.
4. The envoys were seeking peace.
5. We will walk in the sunshine.
6. We will prepare our forces in *the time* of peace.
7. We will fortify the citadel.
8. Poverty is an evil.
9. Freedom is sweet.
10. Dogs' teeth are sharp.
11. The chiefs of the community are coming to Caesar.
12. We will keep the customs of *our* ancestors.
13. Hear *me*, Jupiter.
14. *Some* oxen were lying in a meadow.
15. I will send envoys to the camp of the praetor.
16. Demosthenes was the chief of Grecian orators.
17. Death is the end of all sorrows.
18. The Greeks were the discoverers of many arts.
19. The oxen were dragging the plough.
20. Robbers live in *the midst of* slaughter.

EXERCISE XIII.

CONSONANT-NOUNS—*continued.* § 55 to 63.

Look out pateo ; virtus ; agmen, acies ; scelus, crimen ; accedo.

1. They drag the priest from the altar.
2. The boys are breaking the boughs of the trees.
3. You shall pay the penalty of *your* crimes.
4. The designs of Caesar are manifest.

5. Latona was the mother of Apollo.
6. Proserpina was the daughter of Ceres.
7. Death is the door of life.
8. We are seeking safety by flight.
9. Envy is the companion of merit.
10. Jove will avert the omen.
11. A vast body of women was approaching the city.
12. He will give you many pledges of *his* goodwill.
13. He was sitting by (*ad*) the side of the praetor.
14. I have a headache.
15. The name of peace is sweet.
16. I have a pain *in my* side.
17. The love of wealth increases.
18. We will carry the gift to Juno's altar.
19. A boy was approaching the prison wall.
20. We are waging war with words against weapons.

EXAMINATION PAPER C.

On § 1-66.

1. Write in full the Future Imperfects of gestīre, *to be eager*, prŏdĕre, *to betray*, dēsistĕre, *to cease*, discēdĕre, *to depart*, rŏgāre, *to ask*, dēdĕre, *to surrender*, căvēre, *to be cautious*, stătuĕre, *to set up*, intelligĕre, *to comprehend*.

2. Decline anceps, pauper, equester, motus, nisus, nasus, socer, socrus, domus, spes, signum, *standard*, ĕquĭtātus, *cavalry*, desidia, *sloth*, acies, *battle-array*, *pitched-battle*, delectus, *levy*.

3. What are the Genders and the meanings of manus, domus, meridies, vis, genu, dies, ōs, ŏs, ver, virtus, uxor, dolor ?

4. What are Present Perfects of iubeo, disco, lĕgo, venio, vincio, veho, mitto, fallo ?

5. Decline dives, teres, uber (*fruitful*), pes celer, urbs pulchra, lepus timidus, bos piger.

6. Render in Latin the following phrases :—

ENGLISH.	LATIN.
(1) to pledge *one's* word.	to give faith.
(2) to keep *one's* word.	to preserve faith.
(3) to plead a cause.	to speak a cause.
(4) to conduct a case.	to perform a cause.
(5) to plant a tree.	to sow a tree.
(6) to plant a standard.	to set up a standard.
(7) to practise virtue.	to cultivate virtue.
(8) to entertain hope.	to have hope.
(9) to make a levy.	to hold a levy.
(10) to arrive in the camp.	to come into the camp.
(11) to arrive at Rome.	to come to Rome.
(12) to fight against Pompeius.	to fight with Pompeius.
(13) to marry a wife.	to lead a wife (*i.e.* home).

EXERCISE XIV.

NOUNS WITH *U* AND *E* STEMS. § 64 to 66.

Look out teneo ; fides ; res publica ; ritus ; dolor ; moveo ; res ;
ingenium ; plebs, populus.

1. The ships were steering a straight course.
2. I have a great work in hand (*pl.*).
3. The ships are coming into harbour.
4. I have hope in the *good* faith of Caesar.
5. He has great experience in public affairs.
6. They fight like lions (*Lat.*, in the fashion of wild beasts).
7. Mark the fellow's extravagance.
8. I hear the clashing of arms.
9. The countenance is the portrait of the soul.
10. You will make men laugh (*Lat.*, You will move the smiles of men).
11. The maiden shows signs of grief in her looks.
12. The king was on (in) the right wing.
13. They live like brute-beasts (*Lat.*, sheep).
14. We will cherish the hope of freedom.
15. He will keep *his* word.
16. He will not abide by *his* promise.

17. The issues of wars are uncertain.
18. We shall come to the end of *our* labours.
19 The speeches of the Gracchi used to excite the commons.
20. In many occupations experience is better than genius.

EXERCISE XV.

PERFECT TENSES. § 67 to 73.

Look out instruo; fides; acies, agmen; nefarius; anguis, serpens.

1. The girl wept.
2. The goddess smiled.
3. The snake lay hidden.
4. The consul made a levy.
5. The consul delivered a speech.
6. We have yielded to fortune.
7. The general had marshalled *his* forces.
8. Caesar had left Italy.
9. Pamphilus has married a wife.
10. The slave has kept *his* faith.
11. The praetor has broken his word.
12. Catiline came into the senate.
13. Caesar had sent trusty envoys.
14. Labienus drew up *his* army in battle-array before the town.
15. Caesar had left the baggage in the camp.
16. I had great hope in the honour of Caesar.
17. The son obeyed *his* father.
18. We heard the sound of the trumpet.
19. Cassius, you were envious of me.
20. You have committed a foul crime.

EXERCISE XVI.

PERFECT TENSES—*continued.*   § 67 to 73.

Look out legatus ; pono, facio ; acies ; cornu, ala, penna.

1. We heard the shout of the enemy.
2. Caesar had fortified the camp.
3. They have taken up arms against *their* country.
4. Caesar will come to Rome.
5. Crassus has arrived in Italy.
6. The praetor had left a garrison in the city.
7. I have been obedient to the laws.
8. I lived with Panaetius.
9. I sought the friendship of Caesar.
10. The soldiers had taken up *their* arms.
11. The boy has broken the bow.
12. Marius had left *his* lieutenant in the camp.
13. Romulus had vowed a temple to Jupiter.
14. We sought the rewards of *our* labour.
15. Caesar put a bridge over (in) the river.
16. Aulus had made a treaty with Jugurtha.
17. The river has changed *its* course.
18. Darius built a bridge over the Ister.
19. The Romans vanquished the Gauls in a pitched battle.
20. Caesar had stationed all the cavalry on the wings.

NOTE.— *Observe how frequently a single word in Latin will express two or more words in English : for example :—*

ENGLISH.	LATIN.
I put confidence in.	credo.
I have an affection for.	amo.
in security.	tuto.
step by step.	ordino.
to hope for.	sperare.
to steer for.	petere.
harsh usage.	vis.
an act of injustice.	iniuria.
young people.	iuvenes.
to feel alarm.	timere *or* metuere.
at the present time.	nunc.
to make preparations for.	parare.

EXERCISE XVII.

ADVERBS AND ADVERBIAL EXPRESSIONS. § 74 to 76.

Look out amo, diligo ; pono, expono ; vis, numerus.

1. Soldiers, we will remain here.
2. Caesar placed a garrison there.
3. You will always be a poor *man.*
4. I never liked the man.
5. You seldom write to me.
6. I put but little confidence in you.
7. I have always had an affection for you.
8. You managed the matter well.
9. You managed the matter exceedingly well.
10. Here you will live in security.
11. The river has never changed its course.
12. I do not sufficiently comprehend the matter.
13. He will manage the matter badly.
14. He carried on the war bravely against the enemy.
15. We commend you rightly for *your* merit.
16. I will now explain the matter step by step to you (*pl.*).
17. He has just sent into the town a great quantity of gold.
18. Pompeius did not often attend the senate.
19. The enemy pitched *their* camp at a distance from the city walls.
20. The master praises the boy too much.

EXERCISE XVIII.

ATTRIBUTIVE EXPRESSIONS. § 77, 78.

Look out delictum, vitium, culpa ; paucus ; peto ; Marathonius ;
Plautinus ; Parthicus ; Leuctricus.

1. I beg pardon for *my* fault.
2. The fishes were swimming on the surface of the water.
3. Hippias fell in the battle of Marathon.

4. The general gave the rest of the booty to the soldiers.
5. The rest of the legions arrived in the camp.
6. The Carthaginians sent Hannibal as a commander into Italy.
7. I have sent you a copy of Caesar's letter.
8. At the present time I am in mid-ocean.
9. There was an island in the middle of the river.
10. Titus steered for the island of Cyprus.
11. A few only of the senatorial order sought safety in flight.
12. We read with pleasure the plays of Plautus.
13. Caesar was making preparations for a war with Parthia.
14. The senate sent Lucullus to *conduct* the war against Mithridates.
15. The victorious Romans dash into the enemy's camp with the hope of *getting* booty.
16. Helen was the cause of the Trojan war.
17. The son was the heir to all *his* father's property.
18. He drew up *his* army in battle array half way up the hill.
19. Epaminondas vanquished the Spartans at the battle of Leuctra.
20. Ariovistus, leader of the Helvetii, sent envoys to the camp of Caesar.

EXAMINATION PAPER D.

On PART I.

1. Give instances of the use of the Subjunctive in the Simple Sentence.

2. Give some examples illustrating the use of the Gerunds and the Gerundive.

3. Write some Adverbs of Time and Place.

4. Decline comes, pectus, parens, vis, iudex, quercus, status, *position*, teges, pedes, fur.

5. Decline comis, vetus, pauper, paluster, uber, macer.

6. What are the Genitives, Genders, and meanings of aether, aer, finis, pons, porticus, vulnus, palus, custos, fraus, lex ?

7. What cases do the following prepositions take : extra, de, super, trans, apud ?

8. What are the Perfect tenses of lĕgo, peto, veho, venio, vinco, rideo, curro, duco ?

9. Render in Latin the following phrases :—

ENGLISH.	LATIN.
(1) a wreath of gold.	a golden wreath.
(2) at midnight.	in the middle of the night.
(3) a man of learning.	a learned man.
(4) to travel on foot.	to make a journey with the feet.
(5) the course of events.	use *res.*
(6) the position of affairs.	use *res.*
(7) to put to flight.	to turn into flight.
(8) without consulting Caesar.	without the advice of Caesar.
(9) to be alarmed.	to be in alarm.
(10) to be at ease.	to be in ease.

EXERCISE XIX.

VERBAL NOUNS. § 79 to 85.

Look out dementia, amentia ; peccatum ; prodo ; cibus ; pompa ; Campanus ; causa.

1. Learn to obey the laws.
2. Learn to keep at home.
3. Caesar ordered *his* men to construct a camp.
4. Antonius is eager to destroy the senate.
5. To hope for safety in flight is downright-folly.
6. I was preparing to send letters to Rome.
7. I did not hesitate to seek advice from you by letter.
8. To betray *one's* country is a wicked-thing.
9. Let men cease to fear death.
10. Caesar had forbidden the envoys to depart.
11. The consul ordered his men to take refreshment.
12. I am anxious to see you for many reasons.

13. *My* mother took me to see the procession.
14. The people of Capua have sent us to you as envoys, to ask aid from you.
15. Horsemen came from Suessula to the consul Valerius, to beg for assistance.
16. Our friends bid us be hopeful.
17. We learn by teaching.
18. He had a motive for remaining.
19. Magius was insolvent.
20. The states were bankrupt.

EXERCISE XX.

THE GERUNDIVE. § 86, 87.

Look out virtus ; inimicus, hostis ; committo, proelium ; cogito ; delibero ; spatium ; facultas ; opera, opus ; caveo.

1. We have to dread harsh usage (*Lat.*, violence must be feared by us).
2. Merit ought to be assisted (*Lat.*, assistance must be given to virtue).
3. The valour of the soldiers was deserving of praise.
4. We ought to spare *our* enemies.
5. You must marry a wife.
6. We must seek for peace.
7. I will explain to you *my* plans for carrying on the war.
8. Now *we* must fight.
9. We must fight for Italy.
10. Caesar gave the signal to engage.
11. I will make an end of writing.
12. I will not cease to beg.
13. Believe me, Cassius, I will never cease to think of you.
14. He requested *to have* a day to consider *the matter*.
15. The soldiers had scarcely time (*Lat.*, space) to take up *their* arms.

16. Caesar gave the Helvetii permission to pass through the province.
17. Nature has given us eyes to make manifest the emotions of *our* souls.
18. The consul takes pains to appease the gods.
19. Envoys came from Thyatira to surrender *that* city.
20. By using caution in all *matters* you will be safe.

EXERCISE XXI.

PARTICIPLES, IMPERATIVE AND SUBJUNCTIVE MOODS.   § 88 to 94.

Look out ruo, cado ; dirigo ; invenio ; praecipio ; desero ; clamo ; fortunatus ; discordia, controversia.

1. I saw the wall falling.
2. I heard the girl sing.
3. Deiotarus had intended to come to Rome.
4. The slave was carrying a knife concealed beneath his dress.
5. Pompeius, seeking safety, steered his fleet to the island of Cyprus.
6. Caesar vanquished the Germans that dwelt on the further side of the Rhine.
7. We found Cato asleep.
8. I intend to give you nothing.
9. Decius the consul, while warring against Pyrrhus, king of Epirus, fell in battle.
10. I will obey you when you give me good advice.
11. Fear nothing on my account.
12. The Samnites, while they prepare war, seek for peace.
13. Fear not, I will not forsake thee.
14. Do not cry out too much.
15. Let us avoid the missiles of the enemy.
16. Let us await the issue of the war.

17. I trust I may be a false prophet.
18. Hand the book to the boy.
19. May you all be prosperous !
20. Let there be an end of the disputes.

EXAMINATION PAPER E.

On PART I.

1. Explain the terms Subjective Genitive, Objective Genitive.

2. How are the Supines used ?

3. Decline poema, cinis, caput, pater, lis, nix, iter.

4. Decline celer, saluber, comis, comes, integer, hebes, pauper, iter longum, mos antiquus, testis vivus.

5. What are the Genders of ignis, sal, mel, merces, custos, cos ?

6. What are the Present-Perfect tenses of facio, pono, vincio, sedeo, cado, cedo, sto, parco ?

7. Render in Latin the following phrases and sentences :—

ENGLISH.	LATIN.
(1) to arrive in Rome.	
(2) to arrive in Italy.	
(3) in a cruel way.	cruelly.
(4) in a clever manner.	wisely.
(5) to feel grateful.	to have thanks.
(6) in the hour of death.	in death.
(7) to intrust with the management of the affair.	to give the affair to be carried on (gerundive).

8. The Roman people intrusted Crassus with the management of the war.

9. Caesar's letter will have great weight with me.

10. He spent the night in the woods.

11. Piso arrived in Egypt.

12. I will answer you in a friendly way.

13. I did nothing without consulting the senate.

14. Caesar sent the rest of the legions to the camp.

EXERCISE XXII.—Recapitulatory.

Look out apud ; litterae ; expulsus ; venio.

1. I have a headache.
2. Caesar will keep his word.
3. He has an important work in hand.
4. Look at the man's folly.
5. He has managed the business badly.
6. We have reached the end of *our* labours.
7. I have explained the matter step by step.
8. I expressed my gratitude to Caesar.
9. You have suffered for *your* folly.
10. Pamphilus has married a wife.
11. Caesar vanquished Pompeius near Pharsalus in Thessaly.
12. You have often taken many precautions on my account.
13. You have given yourself up to laziness.
14. The gods waged war against the giants.
15. M. Cato learnt the Greek language in *his* old age.
16. Hannibal, *when* banished from Carthage, went to Ephesus.
17. An honourable death should never be avoided.
18. Labienus came up to the enemy's camp.
19. The timorous hares have sought safety in flight.
20. Pompeius married Cornelia, the daughter of Q. Metellus Scipio.

PART II.

EXERCISE XXIII.

CONJUNCTIONS. § 95 to 102.

Look out gratias ago, gratias habeo ; vis ; facinus ; infans, liberi.

1. The boys and the girls were singing.
2. The horns and the trumpets are sounding.
3. The slaves and the handmaidens obey their master.
4. The leaves of the lilies and roses will fall.
5. The dog watches the sheep and the lambs.

6. The poplar supplies shade for the cows and the calves.
7. We praise the upright and honest man.
8. I thank Piso, and I am grateful *to him*.
9. A sudden and unexpected panic seized the Romans.
10. We fear not severity of cold or heat.
11. Orestes, the son of Agamemnon and Clytemnestra, slew his mother.
12. Titus steered his course for the islands of Rhodes and Cyprus.
13. Cnaeus Pompeius waged war against Mithridates and Tigranes.
14. We live without care and apprehension.
15. Theramenes and Socrates drank poison.
16. You have done an unworthy and bad deed.
17. I call you not to war nor to danger.
18. The boy desires a gift and a reward.
19. He spared neither women nor children.
20. God has neither beginning nor end.

EXERCISE XXIV.

CONJUNCTIONS—*continued.*   § 95 to 102.

Look out inventor ; eruditus ; specto ; consilium ; auctoritas ; traicio.

1. We will plant olives and vines.
2. You speak in a learned and clever way.
3. You give me friendly and sage advice (*use adverbs*).
4. The king is preparing for war by land and by sea.
5. You cherish an ungrounded and deceitful hope.
6. He deceives the foolish and unwary.
7. You deceive our hopes and expectations.
8. Zeno was the founder and the chief of the Stoics.
9. Learning and learned men have always given me pleasure.
10. He grudged neither toil nor risk.

11. He led forth men *armed* with shields and swords.
12. Caesar crossed the river and encamped.
13. The stars have fixed and regular courses.
14. By *my* policy and influence I saved the king and the kingdom.
15. The affair began to wear the appearance of violence and slaughter.
16. We have not given ourselves up to slavery, but *we have trusted* to your honour.
17. Originally (*Lat.*, in the beginning) the Trojans built the city of Rome, and dwelt *therein*.
18. The great-grandfather and the grandfather of L. Murena were praetors.
19. We have vanquished the enemy's forces by land and sea.
20. Juno was the daughter of Saturn and the wife of Jove.

EXERCISE XXV.

CONJUNCTIONS—*continued.* § 95 to 102.

Look out etiam, quoque; consulo; mortuus; guberno; lateo, fugio; conscius; amitto, perdo; autem, sed; nex, mors.

1. Thou too, O mother, wert hard-hearted.
2. He consults me repeatedly.
3. Learn or leave.
4. I do not command, but I advise.
5. We are consulting for (*Lat.*, we seek) the safety not of *our* allies but of Roman citizens.
6. Preserve *your* wives, *your* children, and your fortunes.
7. Protect the name and safety of the Roman people.
8. He lost not only *his* freedom, but *his* life also.
9. *It is* not hope but duty *that* guides us.
10. The soul in *the hour of* death flies away from the chains of the body, as from a prison.
11. I protected myself not with a public guard, but by private watchfulness.

12. Death is either a natural necessity (*Lat.*, a necessity of nature), or an end of toils and troubles.
13. You are not only importunate, but ignorant to boot (also).
14. He states *his* case; he asks for help.
15. Caius Marius pledged his word, but did not keep it (repeat *fides*).
16. The body of one sleeping lies *like that* (ut) of a dead man, whereas the soul is full-of-vigour and life.
17. The king reigns, but he does not rule.
18. I will obey you not only with a patient but with a willing spirit.
19. A father used to have the power of life and death over (in *with acc.*) his sons.
20. Not one of the accomplices escaped, either by concealment or by flight.

EXERCISE XXVI.

PRONOUNS.   § 103, 104.

Look out timor, metus; aetas, tempus; grex; condio, condo.

1. I am Chremes.
2. I devote myself to *the study of history.*
3. You even increase my alarm.
4. You have taken many precautions for me and mine.
5. You set at nought all authority (*pl.*).
6. I am eagerly awaiting your advice.
7. You deceive your countrymen.
8. My countrymen will forgive me.
9. Time (*aetas*) will assuage your grief.
10. Demetrius gave his daughter in marriage to Seleucus.
11. Caecina sent *his* veteran battalions against Vocula and his army.
12. The senate is on our side.
13. I thanked Antonius on your behalf (*Lat.*, in your name).

14. Pompeius keeps in the town; we are encamped (*Lat.*, have a camp) at the gates.
15. Caesar withdrew his troops to the nearest hill.
16. I am paying the penalty of my offence.
17. The Egyptians embalm their dead, and keep them in their houses (*Lat.*, at home).
18. You have managed your business well.
19. The women are bringing with them a troop of waiting-maids.
20. The Sabine farm is mine.

EXERCISE XXVII.

PRONOUNS—*continued.* § 103 to 108.

Look out impetro, obtineo; metuo, timeo; ago; capio; epigramma; numerus; clarus; amitto; perdo.

1. I have lost the book you gave me.
2. You shall obtain that which you ask.
3. I have read the verses you sent me.
4. Soldiers, you have the opportunity you sought.
5. The consuls came to the army that I had in Apulia.
6. I will explain briefly the plan that I have now *in my mind.*
7. I will gladly do *that* which you ask.
8. Whom do I see?
9. From whom (*pl.*) shall I seek aid?
10. What do you fear?
11. You wish for that which you have.
12. I will not hesitate to say what I think.
13. Let us proceed with the plan that we have adopted.
14. Men of Capua, you have the freedom that you sought.
15. The matter, which I am about to mention, is well known.
16. I have sent you a copy of the letter that I wrote to Pompeius.

17. The accounts (*quae*) you heard from Tullia about the young people are true.
18. I will tell you without hesitation what I think.
19. Simonides wrote an inscription for (*in*) the Lacedaemonians who fell at Thermopylae.
20. *He* who cheats *his* partner ought not to be reckoned among (*Lat.*, in the number of) honest men.

EXERCISE XXVIII.

PRONOUNS—*continued*. § 109 to 113.

Look out habeo ; valvae, fores ; legio, cohors, manipulus ; invenio, reperio ; accipio, recipio ; signum.

1. This man keeps your daughters in slavery.
2. Touch the altar of Venus here.
3. Their praise is our blame.
4. Turn yourself this way, *my* lad.
5. Remain thou in this place.
6. The folding-doors opened of their own accord (*se ipsae*).
7. You *are* the very *man* I was looking for.
8. Order those *men* yonder to depart from that spot.
9. Here you will find arms and men.
10. Yonder are *your* standards and your arms.
11. From whom did you receive that letter ?
12. The man that hired me took me off to his house (*Lat.*, led away home).
13. I will seek this additional (*quoque*) reward of *my* toil.
14. That is not my fault, but *the fault* of the times.
15. These doors are always open to *receive* me.
16. I do not see the end of these events.
17. The rule of expediency is the same as that (*quae*) of rectitude.
18. The matter is just as you left it (*Lat.*, in the same position in which you left *it*).
19. This is the man who slew our legions.
20. I will read the speech about which you wrote to me lately.

EXERCISE XXIX.

PRONOMINAL ADJECTIVES. § 114.

Look out peto; alienus; foveo; propinquus, cognatus; vinco, subigo; ratio; consilium; uter, uterque.

1. Seek *for thyself* another farm.
2. He is trying to get the farms of other people (*alienus*) (*fem.*).
3. Thou (*fem.*) alone art pleasing to me.
4. We have no fire.
5. No one will ever believe *it*.
6. He believes nobody.
7. But few fell on both sides.
8. Pompeius has given himself up entirely (*adj.*) to Caesar.
9. Some were dressing *the wounds* of brothers, others the wounds of kinsmen.
10. It is one thing to traduce *a man, and* another to accuse *him*.
11. I have no one here *who is* either (*neque*) a friend or a kinsman.
12. We will take counsel *about* (*genitive*) the whole matter.
13. I find no explanation of the matter.
14. We have conquered the whole of Gaul.
15. He sends back most of *his* ships to Italy.
16. Which of you two will fight me ?
17. Take ye whichever of the two ye prefer (*placet*).
18. He left not one of these statues in Sicily.
19. He has devoted himself entirely (*adj.*) to literature.
20. Most people did not approve this project of Caesar.

EXERCISE XXX.

FINAL CONJUNCTIONS. § 115, 116.

Look out haruspex, augur; specto; valeo; lubenter; rogo, peto, oro.

1. He does this to increase the number of the citizens.
2. He did this to increase the number of the citizens.
3. He was requesting me to defend his son.
4. Nothing prevents me from visiting you.
5. What is there to hinder *us* from driving the tyrant out of the kingdom?
6. I requested Caesar to send a letter to you.
7. Who doubts that the art of soothsayers is *of* divine *origin?*
8. It is indisputable that the authority of augurs is weighty.
9. I will take pains to satisfy you on this subject.
10. Mind you do not fall down into the pit.
11. It is certain that God takes thought for the affairs of men.
12. I cannot doubt that the affair has a warlike look.
13. Who doubts that Caesar regards us as enemies?
14. Cyrsilus advised the Athenians to remain in the city.
15. My affection for you compels me to feel alarm.
16. Take pains to keep yourself in good health.
17. I did not doubt that you would read my letter with pleasure (*lubenter*).
18. I am not so stupid as to say that (*ista*).
19. *My* age prevents my doing that.
20. I do not question the existence of poets before Homer.

EXAMINATION PAPER F.

On § 1-116.

1. What are the rules for the Agreement of the Adjective with its Noun?

2. Decline tu, is, qui, hic, ipse.

3. Decline alius, uter, plerique, nemo, solus, dives, celer.

4. Decline acus, femur, ovis, inops, lis, sus, dux, pedes.

5. Give the Ablative Singular and Genitive Plural of clavis, pauper, avis, arx, celer.

6. What are the Genders of panis, pons, bidens, funis, vulgus, latus, lectus, cos, ros?

7. What are the Perfect tenses of ago, volvo, mitto, sumo, video, disco, iubeo, sto, fallo, sentio?

8. Render in Latin the following phrases and sentences :—

ENGLISH.	LATIN.
(1) one after another.	one over another.
(2) Crassus and I.	I and Crassus.
(3) I went away against my will.	I went away unwilling.
(4) I am entirely devoted to you (*pl.*)	I am entirely (*adj.*) yours.
(5) no good man.	no-one good.
(6) he did it in wrath.	he did *it* angry.
(7) all of us.	we all.
(8) most of us.	
(9) none of us.	no-one of us.
(10) not a word of mine.	use *dictum.*
(11) one word of thine.	use *verbum.*
(12) the men in the citadel.	they who were in the citadel.
(13) most of us shrink from toil.	
(14) you speak not for but against me.	for me.
(15) every one despises you.	all despise you.
(16) I carry all my *property* with me.	my (*neut. pl.*).
(17) he was the only one who said this.	he alone said this.
(18) these things have a natural enmity to each other.	are by nature hostile between themselves.
(19) to be justified in killing.	to slay lawfully.
(20) to devote himself to literature.	to give himself to letters.

EXERCISE XXXI.—Recapitulatory.

Look out voveo ; caput ; ius, lex ; eloquens, disertus ; ratio ; odium.

1. There are no garrisons in the towns.
2. I derive great joy and pleasure from your fame.
3. Your letter raises my hopes greatly (*Lat.*, causes great hope to me).
4. Our commanders have sacrificed their lives for the safety of their country.
5. Would that my brother were still living, and again in command of the fleet !
6. We were not superior to the Gauls in strength, nor to the Carthaginians in cunning.
7. Cratippus came to Ephesus to pay his respects to me (*Lat.*, for the sake of saluting and visiting me).
8. Among the Germans the ministers of justice have the power of life and death.
9. He has violated all human and divine laws by a foul crime.
10. Your conduct gives me extreme pleasure.
11. Libo arrived at Brundisium and occupied the island facing the harbour at Brundisium (*adj.* Brundusinus).
12. The consuls, accompanied by the senate and the city cohorts, had occupied the forum and the capitol.
13. The eye, though it cannot see (*Lat.*, not seeing) itself, perceives other *objects*.
14. In public *matters* nothing has greater weight than a statute ; in private *matters* a will is absolutely binding (*Lat.*, most firm).
15. Asia is a rich and productive *country*.
16. I will not disappoint your opinion of my honesty.
17. It is also useful to make a frequent practice of extempore speaking (*Lat.*, often to speak suddenly).

18. All men speak well enough on a subject with which they are familiar (*Lat.*, in that which they know).
19. I did not keep an account of this money.
20. Themistocles was in bad repute with the Spartans, and with his own countrymen.

EXERCISE XXXII.

DIRECT AND INDIRECT QUESTIONS. § 117, 118.

Look out platea ; caeruleus ; epistola ; nunc, iam.

1. Do you hear nothing ?
2. Where is your son ?
3. Did you do this ? I did.
4. Do you invite me to dinner ? I do.
5. Do you see yonder ship ?
6. Do you not see yonder ship ?
7. Did I send you a letter from Ephesus ?
8. Are those *women* your maid-servants ? They are.
9. Why then is he here ?
10. Where is Antipho at the present moment ?
11. Tell *me* where your wife is.
12. Was Horatius justified in killing his sister ?
13. The question is whether Horatius was justified in killing his sister.
14. I ask who did this besides you.
15. Whence shall I seek assistance ?
16. Who is this old *fellow* whom I see at (*in*) the end of the street ?
17. Is not the sea blue ?
18. I ask what Sextius has done in this matter.
19. Did Lucretia fear death ?
20. Do you compel me to believe these fables ?

EXERCISE XXXIII.

COMPARISON OF ADJECTIVES. § 119 to 125.

Look out usus ; loquax ; amarus ; postremus ; disertus ; modestus ; honos, magistratus.

1. Experience is the best teacher.
2. I never saw a more worthless fellow.
3. Nothing *is* more delightful than this retirement.
4. All your designs are clearer to us than daylight.
5. Old age is naturally somewhat garrulous.
6. Nothing is sweeter than freedom.
7. Old age makes me rather testy.
8. The bravest often fall by the missiles of cowards.
9. An honourable death is more to be desired than a disgraceful life.
10. To be in slavery is the worst (*postremum*) of all evils.
11. Nothing is more agreeable to me than retirement.
12. The camp was admirably suited (*Lat.*, most suitable) for carrying on the war.
13. Among the Syracusans the priesthood of Jove is the most honourable office.
14. I never saw a more disgusting *act*.
15. Your *friend* Celer is more eloquent than wise (use *magis*).
16. I never saw a man in a greater fright (*Lat.*, more disturbed by fear).
17. You will find no one more fit *for the business* than I am.
18. He is more learned than retiring.
19. Art is a surer guide than nature.
20. Disgrace is a worse *evil* than pain.

EXERCISE XXXIV.

COMPARISON OF ADJECTIVES AND ADVERBS.

§ 119 to 125.

Look out vis ; pro ; licentia ; efficio ; scio, nosco ; deterior, peior ;
antiquus, vetus.

1. We have managed the business very foolishly.
2. I state this confidently.
3. Your letters amuse me vastly.
4. I love Brutus no less than you (*do*).
5. I love Brutus no less than (*I love*) you.
6. The gods diffuse their influence far and wide.
7. He defended *his* life very stoutly against (*ab*) his foes.
8. Pomponius pleased me immensely.
9. For a very long time I have heard nothing of you.
10. He used to speak with more boldness than skill.
11. He will master you with the greatest ease.
12. Europe is smaller than Asia.
13. It is better to be ignorant of the future (*Lat.*, those things which are about to be) than to know *it*.
14. The most finished of the orations of Demosthenes is *that* in defence of Ctesiphon.
15. The taint of that wickedness extends further than you imagine.
16. Who is more blessed than you ?
17. All *of us* are the worse for the want of control.
18. Does pleasure make (*efficere*) a man better or more praiseworthy ?
19. This fellow is the most worthless of all that are, that have been, that are yet to come.
20. No one is an older friend of mine (*dat.*) than you.

EXERCISE XXXV.

NUMERALS. § 126 to 128.

Look out ago ; via ; Imperator, Princeps ; pedes, eques.

1. Priamus, king of Troy, had fifty sons.
2. Caesar sent four legions to Placentia.
3. I am now in *my* eightieth year (use *ago*).
4. Two hundred on the side of (*ab*) the Romans, eight hundred of the enemy fell.
5. Has Antipho two wives ?
6. Hannibal sent back to *their* homes more than (*supra*) seven thousand men.
7. The number of the prisoners was seven thousand two hundred.
8. The third legion set the example to the other legions of Maesia.
9. He left thirteen farms.
10. I am now in my sixty-fourth year.
11. I *was the* first *to* discover this method.
12. Augustus received the title of Imperator twenty-one times.
13. Full (*ad*) six thousand men *were* slain : two thousand five hundred *were* taken prisoners.
14. Cn. Pompeius *was the* first of the Romans *that* subdued the Jews.
15. Such was the end of his life, in the thirty-seventh year of his age.
16. Gallus was leading the first legion to the relief of Placentia.
17. Pick out men from all the infantry and cavalry, a hundred of each.
18. Vocula adds to his army a thousand men picked from the fifth and fifteenth legions.

19. The cause of the second Punic war, which Hannibal waged with (*contra*) the Romans, was the siege of Saguntum.
20. He sent thirteen thousand eight hundred and fifty foot-soldiers to Africa.

EXERCISE XXXVI.

SPACE AND TIME. § 130 to 134.

Look out iter ; condo ; vallum, vallus ; hortus ; sacculum ; hiberna.

1. He reached the territories of the Nervii by forced marches (*Lat.*, great journeys).
2. He reigned *but* a few months.
3. The field has been fallow for many years.
4. He set about constructing (*Lat.*, arranged to make) ditches thirty feet in width (*accusative*).
5. Homer and Hesiod lived (*fuerunt*) before the foundation of Rome.
6. Virtue must never at any time (*Lat.*, at no time) be abandoned.
7. Diodorus has lived many years in our house (*locative*).
8. Homer lived many generations before Hesiod.
9. The winter quarters of Crassus were twenty-five miles from Caesar's camp (use *absum*).
10. Tarquinius Superbus reigned five-and-twenty years.
11. He completed an earth-work eighty feet high.
12. Caesar weighed anchor at sunset.
13. Since that time Mithridates has reigned twenty-two years (*Lat.*, is now reigning the twenty-third year).
14. The Romans stood in battle-array from sunrise till late in the day.
15. The Nervii surrounded *their* winter quarters with a rampart nine feet *high* and a ditch fifteen feet *wide*.

16. In this workshop he was wont to sit for a great part of the day.
17. He invited the man to his gardens to dinner for the following day.
18. Cato died (*excedere e vita*) at the age of eighty-five years.
19. On the river he had built (*efficere*) two bridges, with a space of four miles between them (*distantes inter se*).
20. Livius exhibited a play about 410 years after the foundation of Rome, the year before the birth of Ennius.

EXAMINATION PAPER **G.**

On § 1-125.

1. What are the Primary and Historic tenses of the verb *mitto* ?

2. What are the rules for the use of -ne, num, and nonne respectively in direct questions ?

3. Give the Degrees of Comparison of felix, pulcher, novus, sacer, senex, utilis, frugi.

4. Compare the Adverbs facile, audacter, bene, male, diu, saepe, post, ultra.

5. Decline pedes, celer, iter, domus, supellex.

6. Decline vis, vir, hic, metus, quercus, quies, ius, salus, urbs, unus.

7. What are the Perfect tenses of fleo, noceo, cedo, credo, invideo, parco, servio, sino ? Which of these verbs take a Dative of the object ?

8. Render in Latin the following phrases and sentences :—

ENGLISH.	LATIN.
(1) the famous Medea.	
(2) the brave Manlius.	
(3) the learned Pythagoras.	superlative.
(4) the cruel Cinna.	of all most cruel.
(5) what a good-for-nothing fellow !	homo.

ENGLISH.	LATIN.
(6) what a brave fellow !	vir.
(7) he is more bold than brave.	
(8) with your usual courtesy.	which is your courtesy.
(9) with more courage than suc- cess.	comparative adverbs.
(10) a resolute man.	brave.
(11) a nervous man.	timorous.
(12) how did that *notion* come into your head ?	to you into your mind.
(13) Bibulus, I hear, will be in no hurry to depart.	somewhat slow in departing.
(14) the features of the mind are fairer than those of the body.	lineaments.
(15) I hoped for better *results*, but you saw further *than I did*.	saw more.
(16) such was the end of Galba.	such an end had Galba.
(17) never at any time.	at no time.
(18) keep where you are.	
(19) by our own fault.	
(20) do not fear death.	

EXERCISE XXXVII.

ADVERBIAL EXPRESSIONS OF TIME. § 135.

Look out mutuus ; Tusculanum ; tectum ; hiemps, bruma.

1. Come in the morning.
2. To-morrow I will see you.
3. I will wait here till noon.
4. Dolabella was with me this morning (*Lat.*, to-day in the morning).
5. The next day Pompeius struck his camp at daybreak.
6. To-morrow I will lend (*Lat.*, give on loan) you the money that you want.
7. Wild beasts leave *their* lairs at night ; they sleep during the day.
8. On the following day, in the morning, he draws up his forces in front of the camp.

9. With the dawn of day the enemy's cavalry comes up to *our* camp and commences an engagement with our horsemen.

10. Brutus came to his-house-at-Tusculum yesterday: so he will see me to-day.

11. Lepidus sent me a letter yesterday evening from Antium, where he was staying (*Lat.*, for he was there), for he has the house which we sold.

12. Before *it was* light we arrived at the temple of Venus.

13. Milo arrived in the city at midnight.

14. Dionysius himself came to us on the evening of the same day.

15. I was all that time (*abl.*) at Neapolis.

16. At nightfall he sends the whole of the cavalry to the camp of the enemy.

17. I received many of your letters at the same time (*Lat.*, at one time).

18. He kept his army under shelter there for the greater part of the winter.

19. At that time Brutus was staying with me.

20. I write (*perf.*) these *lines* to you on my birthday.

EXERCISE XXXVIII.

TEMPORAL CONJUNCTIONS. § 136.

Look out custodio ; fluvius, amnis ; ardeo, uro ; appeto ; obsido ; consumo ; obligo, obstringo, vincio ; calamus.

1. I will inspect the pleasure-grounds when I come (*fut. perf.*).

2. I will write to you when I have seen Caesar (*fut. perf.*).

3. On my arrival at this place I read your letter.

4. We lose the substance (*Lat.*, certain *things*) while we seek the shadow (*Lat.*, uncertain *things*).

5. Yesterday, when I was at Corinth, I received a letter from you.
6. When they commend you they thank me.
7. While you were sleeping I was keeping guard over you.
8. When I was in camp by the river Pyramus, I received two letters from you at the same time.
9. When Servius was staying with me, Cephalio arrived with your letter.
10. The king, on getting sight of the standards of the enemy, led forth his own (*ipse*) forces also.
11. While those transactions were going on at Rome, the Etrurians were already besieging Sutrium.
12. While the temple of Vesta was on fire, Caecilius Metellus, the Pontifex Maximus, snatched the sacred *vessels* from the flames (*ex incendio*).
13. The spring was already close at hand when Hannibal moved out of winter quarters.
14. When Caesar had finished speaking, Cato made a speech.
15. Hasdrubal, seeing that he must fight, arranges the elephants in the van in front of the standards.
16. Before I commenced the siege of Syracuse, I tried *to make* peace (use *tempto* or *tento*).
17. Ere I saw the province or the camp, fortune bound me to you.
18. In the eighth year after his arrival in Spain Cn. Scipio was slain, on the 29th day after his brother's death.
19. While these things were going on in Africa, Hannibal wasted the summer in the district of Tarentum (*adj. Tarentinus*).
20. When I had determined to write to you, and had taken up my pen, Batonius came to me and handed me your letter.

EXERCISE XXXIX.

PRICE AND VALUE. § 137.

Look out ceteri; aedes; colo; mina; as; modius; vectigal.

1. I sell my corn for no higher price than the rest *of the merchants.*
2. For how much did you sell the farm?
3. At what price is this field to be valued?
4. This man sold his country for gold (*abl.*).
5. You sold the whole state for the price of a province.
6. I hold no one of the nobility in higher esteem.
7. You purchase pleasure with pain.
8. Eriphyle sold her husband's (*vir*) life for gold.
9. What did you give Hortensius for the house?
10. I had a very high regard for your father; and he had a wonderful (*adv.*) respect and affection for me.
11. He sold the boy for twenty minae.
12. This field is not dear at three hundred minae.
13. You bought the horse at your own risk for thirty minae.
14. In a time of dearth M. Seius let the people have (*Lat.,* gave to the people) *corn* at an as for the peck.
15. He bought the house for almost half as much again as its worth (*Lat.,* dearer almost by half than he valued it).
16. For pay and reward you have impaired the dignity of the state.
17. I sold *him* the house at his own price.
18. They have bought up all the taxes for a small sum.
19. I make but little account of you.
20. All the risks of death and banishment must be held (*ducere*) of little account.

EXERCISE XL.

THE ROMAN CALENDAR. § 138 to 143.

Look out lustro ; iter, via ; dare litteras ; hora ; autem, sed.

1. I arrived at Brundisium on the 5th of August.
2. We reached Actium on the 15th of June.
3. We came to Ephesus on the 22d of July.
4. We reached Tarsus on the 5th of June.
5. We arrived at Brundisium on the 25th of November.
6. I came to Laodicea on the last day of July.
7. Hortensius paid me a visit on the 12th of June.
8. On the 30th of August I reviewed the army near Iconium.
9. Tiberius was born (*natus est*) on the 16th of November.
10. Agricola was born on the 13th of June : he died (*excedere*) in *his* 56th year, on the 23d of August.
11. *My* brother Quintus left (*discedere ex*) Asia on the 30th of April, and reached Athens on the 15th of May.
12. Here on the 13th of October we slew a great number of the enemy.
13. This is the 15th of July.
14. I have received your letter dated the 19th of July.
15. I was on my way (*iter facere*) to Laodicea on the 3d of August, when I posted this letter to the camp in Lycaonia.
16. I am writing these lines on the 24th of November at 3 A.M. (*Lat.*, I was writing).
17. I arrived at Astura on the 25th of August, having rested (*Lat.*, *for* I had rested) three hours at Lanuvium to avoid the heat (*Lat.*, on account of the heat).
18. I determined, as I sent you word before, to stay at Lanuvium the day after the Ides.

19. I received three letters of yours on the 14th of April (use *postridie*) : they were dated the 2d, 3d, and 4th (connect the sentences with *autem*).

20. On the 28th of March I arrived at Rome, about 5 P.M.

EXAMINATION PAPER H.

On Parts I. *and* II.

1. What are the ordinary uses of *dum* and *donec?*
2. What are the rules for expressing Time and Price?
3. Decline unus, duo, trecenti.
4. Write in Latin—
   (1) Twenty ships.
   (2) Two hundred ships.
   (3) Three hundred and seven miles.
   (4) In the six hundred and forty-first year.
5. Decline miser, carcer, pauper, vir, vis, bos.
6. What are the Perfect-Past tenses of lego, vivo, vinco, iubeo, gero, scribo, faveo, sto?
7. Compare the Adverbs formed from fortis, bonus, diligens, audax, acer, sapiens.
8. Decline ego, is, quis (*indefinite*), hic.
9. Render in Latin the following phrases and sentences :—

English.	Latin.
(1) ten years hence.	
(2) within the last ten years.	in these ten years.
(3) under thirty years of age.	less than.
(4) for more than four hours.	amplius.
(5) over two months.	plus.
(6) at eleven A.M.	
(7) at ten P.M.	hour of the night.
(8) more and more every day.	
(9) to answer briefly.	in a short *way.*
(10) it is worth while.	there is a pay of work.
(11) two successive kings.	in succession (*adv.*).
(12) throughout *his* reign.	through all the time of *his* reign.
(13) he was in his eighteenth year.	

(14) I was looking for a letter from you day after day.   your letter day from day.

(15) I regard you as a brother.   use *duco* and *locus*.

(16) he begged me to come and unite *my* forces *to his*.   join forces.

(17) I shall be out of town after the 5th of January.   from the 5th.

(18) the man that puts down M. Antonius will put an end to the war.   future perfect.

(19) this day for the first time truth has raised her voice against calumny.   has sent.

(20) thus two successive kings, in different ways, the one by war, the other by peace, increased *the power of* the state.   (*alius alia via*).

EXERCISE XLI.—Recapitulatory.

Look out commilito, contubernalis ; diligo ; passus ; lex ; parum.

1. Have you heard nothing of your mother-in-law ?
2. You have to fight, soldiers, with the men you vanquished by land and by sea in the former war.
3. Crassus smiled but once in his life.
4. Caesar demanded six hundred hostages.
5. Tullus Hostilius reigned thirty-two years.
6. I am writing these lines at 9 P.M. on the 25th of January.
7. Tiberius was born on the 16th of November.
8. What are you about, comrades ? I am yours, and you *are* mine.
9. The armies were not more than half a mile from each other.
10. I, as you know, have always held Dionysius in esteem, but I take a higher estimate of his worth daily.
11. Why is it disgraceful to learn that which it is honourable to know ?
12. No man has lived too short a life who has lived a good life.

13. What is there to hinder Caesar from being happy ?
14. What is there to prevent us doing this ?
15. He, who removes one statute, weakens the rest.
16. Marcus Fabius lived to a great age.
17. I have no doubt about your wish that we should be together.
18. Sophocles composed tragedies when he was very old (*Lat.*, to extreme old age).
19. I have asked Caesar to come to Rome.
20. I asked Caesar to come to Rome.

PART III.

EXERCISE XLII.

SUM AND ITS COMPOUNDS. § 144 to 151.

Look out prosum ; supersum ; nemo ; valetudo ; consilium : desum ; perculsus, abiectus.

1. Your son is not with me (use *absum*).
2. I myself will be with you on the march, *and* in the battle (use *adsum*).
3. About daybreak the consul came up with the cavalry.
4. At the present time books give me no pleasure (*nihil prosunt*).
5. The Athenians had nothing left but their ships.
6. Caesar hurries up to take part in the battle.
7. Your letters are of very great weight with me.
8. I can refuse nothing to the wretched and the suffering.
9. Can we surpass Plato in eloquence ?
10. I have no slave of that name (use *nemo*).
11. Habitus was a man of delicate constitution (*Lat.*, weak health).
12. That affair will be creditable to Cato.
13. We shall be a laughing-stock for the enemy.
14. The barbarians were not deficient in strategy.
15. We have no fellowship with tyrants.
16. This *policy* will always be of advantage to the State.

17. I cannot write more, my spirits are so downcast and desponding.
18. There was a deficiency of all things that were serviceable for repairing the ships.
19. The name of that disease is covetousness (*nom.*).
20. My name is Arcturus (*dat.*).

EXERCISE XLIII.

SUM AND ITS COMPOUNDS—*continued.*   § 144 to 151.

Look out summus; celebritas; splendor; odium; alter.

1. M. Cato has lost *his* son, a *youth* of brilliant parts *and* sterling worth (use *summus* for both epithets).
2. You have a first-rate memory.
3. I cannot bear a crowd *of visitors.*
4. Two legions were *told off* to guard the baggage.
5. A head was wanting to the powerful body.
6. The ships under Nasidius (*adj. Nasidienus*) were of no use, and they quickly withdrew from the fight.
7. P. Crassus was *a man* of very high repute (*splendor*) among the Roman knights.
8. Agesilaus was low in stature, small in person, and lame in one foot.
9. He has left no one to compare with him in merit (*Lat.,* of equal virtue).
10. In all *his* undertakings (*res*) Cato displayed remarkable diligence.
11. Thales *was* the only one among the Seven Sages that was not at the head of affairs in his State.
12. I have a strong-objection (*odium*) to going to bed (*Lat.,* to sleep).
13. I will not fail to write to you (*Lat.,* my letters shall not fail you).
14. The voice of Aeschines was melodious and clear (*sum* with *abl.*).

15. Slaves have the same habits as their masters (*Lat.*, which their masters *have*).
16. A good orator must have been an attentive listener (*Lat.*, receive many things in *his* ears).
17. I shall be the cause (*fuero*) of ruin to all my *friends*.
18. The reason why (*idcirco*) we are all subservient to the laws, *is* that we may be free *men*.
19. The city is a defence and an ornament to the State.
20. Apollonius was of great service to me in many matters *of business*.

EXAMINATION PAPER I.

On § 1-151.

1. State some of the peculiar grammatical constructions with *sum*.
2. How are the Supines used?
3. Write the Subjunctive tenses of possum.
4. Decline celer, anceps, acer, sospes, par, victrix.
5. Decline filia, frigus, hiemps, quis, Iuppiter, arx, lis, imber, nix.
6. What are the Perfect tenses of do, indulgeo, capio, condo, consulo, divido, incipio?
7. Give the Gender, Genitives, and Ablatives Singular of domus, mus, civis, fons, quies, caespes, trabs, lis, tus.
8. Compare diversus, integer, nequam, satis, celer, magnus, malus.
9. Render in Latin the following phrases and sentences :—

ENGLISH.	LATIN.
(1) the loss of children.	to lose children.
(2) it is a wise thing.	it is *the part* of a wise man.
(3) it is a foolish thing.	use *stultitia*.
(4) it is downright folly.	use *amentia*.
(5) it is madness.	use *dementia*.
(6) as soon as I could.	
(7) at a later time.	
(8) at some length.	in more words.

(9) to dine with Caesar.	*apud.*
(10) the best authorities.	the authority of the wisest men
(11) that which is at hand.	
(12) that which is now present.	
(13) we cannot alter the past.	neuter plural.
(14) loss of children is a misfortune.	an evil.
(15) I have lost a day.	*perdo.*
(16) I thanked Caesar at some length.	
(17) I happened to dine that day with Pompeius.	*casu.*
(18) One of the consuls.	*alter.*
(19) from childhood.	from a boy.
(20) to take part with Caesar.	*facio.*

EXERCISE XLIV.

PASSIVE VERBS. § 157 to 162.

Look out vexo, ango, crucio ; urgeo ; celebro ; saepio, claudo ; frango ; neco ; ferrum ; diligo.

1. The ungodly are racked with disquietude.
2. The enemy were receiving reinforcements (*Lat.*, the forces of the enemy were being increased).
3. Messengers were sent to Caesar (*use the Past Imperfect*).
4. Syracuse was founded by the Corinthians.
5. On a sudden the cavalry are perceived in the rear.
6. The seventh legion was hard pressed by the enemy.
7. Nero was feared : Titus was loved.
8. Our house is thronged *with visitors.*
9. All things were being laid waste with fire and sword.
10. I am charmed with your letter.
11. Men are often terrified by false reports.
12. It is better to suffer defeat with the one, than to gain a victory with the other.
13. I am compelled to be a participator, and a partner, and an assistant in this war (*genitive*).
14. The forum will be blocked up; all the approaches will be closed.

15. The messengers were put to death with torture before the eyes of our soldiers.
16. This grief *of mine*, so far from being relieved, is even increased.
17. In all the speeches of Cato every kind of oratorical excellence is found (*Lat.*, all oratorical merits).
18. The attack of the enemy was slightly checked.
19. The walls of the city were shaken with the battering-ram (*use the Past Imperfect*).
20. Not a word (*littera*) is *to be* found in their books about curbing (*frangere*) the passions.

EXERCISE XLV.

DEPONENT VERBS.　§ 163 to 170.

Look out tutor, tueor; regula, norma; forum; utor; potior, occupo; pastus, victus.

1. They are trying to make a fire from green logs.
2. The consul ordered the praetor to defend the sea-coast.
3. Follow me.
4. Let us commence from the beginning.
5. The consuls shared the provinces between them.
6. Let us test our desires by the standard of nature.
7. You were born not for me, not for yourself, but for *your* country.
8. Plato died *while* writing in *his* eighty-first year.
9. Clodius set out from Rome on the preceding day, in order that in front of his own farm he might arrange an ambuscade for Milo.
10. Hortensius *when* quite a youth began to speak in public (*Lat.*, in the forum).
11. The ship, which has the services of (*Lat.*, uses) the most skilful pilot, accomplishes *her* voyage (*Lat.*, course) in the best manner.

12. All men naturally follow *after* the things that seem *to be* blessings, and avoid the opposites.

13. Caesar got possession of a great number of cattle and men too.

14. The Epicureans make pleasure the standard of measurement for (*Lat.*, measure by pleasure) the things which are to be sought for by a man.

15. Octavius is planning great *attempts*.

16. Some creatures approach their food by walking, some by creeping, some by flying, *and* some by swimming.

17. I admit my mistake.

18. I used to respect you as an elder brother.

19. Tiberius Gracchus attempted to take possession of kingly power.

20. Nature bestowed on this man an unbounded flow and readiness of speech (*gerund*).

EXERCISE XLVI.

FERO **AND ITS COMPOUNDS.**   § 174 to 175.

Look out quiesco ; fruges, fructus ; effero, confero, refero, defero ; commodum.

1. He deferred the matter till the following day.

2. Land which has lain fallow for many years is wont to produce more abundant crops.

3. Bibulus did not stir a step from his house.

4. Let us wage war on Italy by land and sea.

5. I will carry out that which I have undertaken.

6. I will produce witnesses to this fact (*res*).

7. He shifted the whole blame on others.

8. Clodius took away the consular provinces from the senate.

9. The son could not endure the abominable deceitfulness of *his* father.

10. Among the Germans *it is* not the wife *that* bestows a marriage-portion on the husband, but the husband on the wife.
11. Aeschines, on withdrawing from Athens, betook himself to Rhodes.
12. I laid the matter before the people.
13. He will shift the whole blame on my shoulders.
14. Compare this peace with that war.
15. I have bestowed all my care and attention on philosophy.
16. I am transported with the desire of seeing you.
17. He thought the welfare of the country of more importance than his own interests.
18. A storm drove the vessel to Cyrenae.
19. He offered himself cheerfully to death.
20. The south-wind carried me back to Italy.

EXERCISE XLVII.

EO AND ITS COMPOUNDS. § 176 to 178.

Look out vesper ; ineo, adeo, obeo, subeo ; vitium, culpa ; atque.

1. The envoy came back from Delphi to Rome.
2. Cleomenes was unwilling to return to Sparta.
3. Pompeius has gone back to the sea.
4. I cannot pass this over in silence (*adj.*).
5. Our men did not hesitate to cross the river.
6. I will not allow you to depart.
7. I will go into the country, and there I will remain (use *atque*).
8. Towards evening Caesar ordered the gates to be closed and the troops to leave the town.
9. The Gauls are beginning to form plans for a war secretly.
10. The ships are gone out of sight.
11. I will return to the place which I left (*illuc unde*).
12. He was unwilling to run the risk.

13. He passed away without a pang.
14. Sulpicius died on *his* embassy.
15. We must all die (use *gerundive* of *obeo*).
16. I am undone by my own fault (*vitium*).
17. Scipio and Afranius have perished miserably.
18. I am reconciled to Caesar.
19. I intend to go home to-morrow.
20. I shall have to pay the same penalty (use *subeo*).

EXERCISE XLVIII.

UNIPERSONAL VERBS. § 181 to 183.

Look out tribunus ; laboro ; voluntas ; plebs ; res publica, civitas.

1. I am sorry for you, my father.
2. Lead me where *you* will.
3. It was thought that Sulpicius would be a candidate for the tribuneship of the commons.
4. The country has an immense interest in this matter.
5. There is not a pin to choose between you and Catiline.
6. There is an enormous difference between the two things (*Lat.*, this and that).
7. You ought to have paid the money.
8. You ought not to have entered the Capitol.
9. It is said that Pompeius is extremely ill.
10. You have done your duty ; it is now incumbent on me to do mine.
11. It is reported to me that your runaway slave is at Vardacum.
12. All men have an interest in being honest.
13. I am sorry for the woman.
14. It is of great importance to me that we should be together.
15. Were you not ashamed to act in that way ?
16. My advice should have prevailed.

17. I shall never regret my intention : I do regret *my* advice.
18. It was clearly to the advantage of the country that Vitellius should be defeated.
19. This ought to have been done long ago.
20. You ought to have upheld the authority of the senate.

EXAMINATION PAPER J.

On § 1-184.

1. Write the Subjunctive tenses in full of partior, utor, and patior.

2. Explain the uses of the Gerunds and the Gerundive.

3. What are the Perfects of gradior, morior, metior, ordior, nanciscor ?

4. What are the Past Perfects of fallo, sto, lĕgo, mitto, relinquo, vivo, vinco ?

5. Mention some Deponent Verbs that take an ablative of the object.

6. Decline in the Singular deus, nullus, vis, impar, iubar, pes, pedes, eques, poples.

7. Give the Gender and Ablative Plural of specus, lis, peristroma, genu, arcus, culter, imber, lacus.

8. Compare felix, maturus, recte, antiquus, senex.

9. Render in Latin the following phrases and sentences :—

English.	Latin.
(1) judge for yourself.	use your judgment.
(2) to be starved to death.	to be killed by hunger.
(3) to improve a victory.	to use a victory.
(4) to reap the fruits of a victory.	to enjoy a victory.
(5) of humble parentage.	born in an obscure station.
(6) of an equestrian family.	
(7) to suffer loss.	to make loss.
(8) do as you please.	you, as it seems *good.*
(9) you were afraid I should not do my duty.	use *desum.*
(10) he set out from Rome.	*proficiscor.*
(11) they are talking to themselves.	three words.
(12) I wish you were in-good-health.	three words.

ENGLISH.	LATIN.
(13) I am on most intimate terms with Caesar.	three words.
(14) for many years I have been very intimate with Trebonius.	*valde familiariter.*
(15) all on a sudden.	suddenly.
(16) with your permission.	use *pax.*
(17) of my own free will.	
(18) all of you.	
(19) two hundred of us.	
(20) the men in the boats.	

EXERCISE XLIX.—Recapitulatory.

Look out fortuna, sors ; gaza ; versor ; patior, sino ; avunculus, patruus.

1. I have no doubt about his having a bitter hatred of me.
2. You were not sorry for your fortune, were you ?
3. Marcus Marcellus, who had been consul three times, was drowned at sea.
4. Catiline could endure cold, thirst, and hunger.
5. Decius devoted himself to death of his own free will.
6. Lentulus the consul takes part with Caesar.
7. I fear the enemy will take the city.
8. Why do you stone me ?
9. We have the best authorities on our side.
10. You act against your professions and promises (*contra quam*).
11. That which we promise for (*de*) Cn. Pompey, he will carry out most honourably.
12. The remembrance and the fame of your kindnesses to us will never pass away (*Lat.*, die).
13. Paulus got possession of all the treasure of the Macedonians.
14. Leisure gives me an opportunity of learning, and you an opportunity of teaching.
15. A cloud was rising out of Vesuvius.
16. You ask me to send you an account of the end of my uncle, in order that you may transmit a more correct account of it to posterity.   I thank *you.*

17. I intend to set out for Rome to-day.
18. He began to form schemes for setting the country free.
19. I agree with you on the subject of preserving freedom, than which nothing is more charming.
20. You cannot now any longer have intercourse with us : I will not bear it, I will not endure it, I will not per-mit it.

EXERCISE L.

ON THE TABLE OF VERBS.   § 185—First Conjugation.

Look out mico ; Falernus ; custodia ; petitio ; comitium, comitia.

1. Labienus gave the signal for battle.
2. The Gauls gave hostages to Caesar.
3. Forgive me.
4. You can help us much with Plancus.
5. Hand washes hand.
6. Swords were flashing.
7. The door rattled (*pl.*).
8. Be off to bed.
9. The veins and arteries do not cease to throb.
10. They have neither the power nor the will to help us.
11. The line of battle resounded with the songs (*sing.*) of the men.
12. We will drink Falernian wine.
13. The fidelity of *our* allies had remained unshaken to that day (*Lat.*, stood firm).
14. You will suffer for your recklessness.
15. You have put yourself in prison.
16. Fortune has given you an end of your toils on this spot (*Lat.*, here).
17. We are taught by the influence of the laws to keep our passions under control.
18. I will help you in *your* canvass with all my influence.

19. Pompeius had given orders that the camp should not be protected by a rampart (use *veto*).
20. The statue of Horatius stood in the Comitium quite within (*ad*) our memory.

EXERCISE LI.

TABLE OF VERBS—Second Conjugation.

Look out iniuria ; ardeo ; caveo ; cunctus ; dolor ; maneo ; valeo ; suadeo, persuadeo ; ulterior ; potio.

1. I will protect you from injustice.
2. I am an enthusiast in the study of history.
3. By exercising caution in all matters you will be safe (*four words*).
4. Forty-four minae are due to me.
5. Caius Marius on his return almost destroyed the whole of the senate (use *cunctus*).
6. Most of the young men favoured the designs of Catiline.
7. The father was bewailing the death of *his* son, the son *the death* of *his* father.
8. *Your* friends are afflicted by your trouble.
9. *There is* nothing *that* remains constantly unchanged (*Lat.*, in its own position).
10. Piso did not swerve from *his* fidelity (use *maneo*).
11. My ears have always been open to the precepts and warnings of all *men*.
12. What good *man* does not lament the death of Trebonius ?
13. I promise you this, my *dear* Cicero.
14. The Gauls were occupying the further bank with an armed force (*Lat.*, with arms).
15. Your authority has very great influence with me.
16. The Decii devoted themselves for the preservation of the country.

17. Mind you are not caught; take heed you are not deceived.
18. Old age has increased my longing for conversation; it has taken away *my appetite* for food and drink.
19. I was the first to advise peace.
20. Ye made no promise to the enemy.

EXAMINATION PAPER K.

On § 1-184.

1. Write the Subjunctive tenses of moneo, cupio, audio.
2. Write the Future tenses, Active and Passive, of rego and audio.
3. Decline grex, ōs, amans, totus, anceps, asper, caro, sal, sol.
4. Decline iste, duo, centeni, quis (indefinite), alius, alter.
5. Compare acer, vetus, diu, malus, iuvenis.
6. What are the Future Perfect tenses of vinco, facio, scribo, venio, rideo, capio, do?
7. What Cases follow the Prepositions pro, praeter, ob, super, apud?
8. Render in Latin the following phrases and sentences:—

ENGLISH.	LATIN.
(1) as I am writing.	as I was writing.
(2) when I had written thus far.	when I had reached this place.
(3) with or without thee.	
(4) to bring to trial.	to call to law.
(5) such is the case.	the matter has itself so.
(6) of his own free will.	look out *sponte*.
(7) to lose a battle.	to be conquered in a battle.
(8) a few days before.	ablative.
(9) many days after.	ablative.
(10) about the same time.	per.
(11) I will not disappoint your expectations.	*opinio*.
(12) he will come before he is expected.	quicker than expectation.
(13) every one will despise you.	
(14) self-love is natural to all men.	love themselves.

ENGLISH.	LATIN.
(15) he is just what he always was.	*idem qui.*
(16) I will ask Caesar to send you a copy of the letter.	
(17) I would rather be at Athens than at Rome.	
(18) do you not pity me?	
(19) I will take Cato as an authority.	*utor.*
(20) I have for a long time desired.	long ago I desire.

EXERCISE LII.

TABLE OF VERBS—Third Conjugation, *B, C, D* Stems.

Look out lăbor ; humanitas, comitas ; abdo ; maritimus ; sido ; ingenium.

1. The she-wolf was licking the boys with her tongue.
2. A state waxes great by industry (*labor*) and justice.
3. Valeria is going to be married to Decimus Brutus.
4. Crassus learnt *all* that could be learnt about law.
5. Know thyself.
6. I know your courtesy (*perfect*).
7. You have given me fresh spirit by commending my books (*Lat.*, added spirits to me).
8. Clodius hid himself in the inner part of the house (*acc.*).
9. Servilius Ahala slew Spurius Maelius with his own hand.
10. It appears to me that Caesar is closing the outlets by sea (*adj.*).
11. The province must be protected from the fear of disaster.
12. He fell from (*ex*) *his* horse and hurt his side badly.
13. I am paying a very severe penalty for my recklessness.
14. A mist had settled on the plain.
15. The ship began to sink.
16. Are we going to play ? (*use the supine.*)
17. Our *friend* Posidonius has published five books on Divination.
18. The number of the enemy increases day by day.

19. Plato, by his writings, has immortalised (*Lat.*, delivered to immortality) the genius of Socrates.
20. What hast thou learnt, my son?

EXERCISE LIII.

TABLE OF VERBS—Third Conjugation, *G, H, I* Stems.

Look out figo; iungo; animus; anima; magnes; heres; diligo.

1. May the god approve, Quirites, *that* which ye are doing, and *that which* ye are about to do.
2. The weapons of the gods are planted in the thoughts of the ungodly.
3. I was the first to break the statutes of Antonius (*adj.*).
4. Deiotarus used to contract intimacies and friendships with our people (*homines*).
5. I have read and I am *still* reading your book carefully (*use the passive*).
6. Subsequently Gabinius broke the league; Piso, however, remained faithful.
7. The soul governs and directs the body.
8. Serious reports have been spread about you.
9. I did it under the compulsion (*part. pass.*) of force and constraint.
10. I always had a high regard for Dionysius.
11. The praetor rose from (*de*) his seat and went away.
12. We are all influenced (*Lat.*, drawn) by the desire for praise.
13. The magnet is a stone which attracts and draws to itself iron.
14. The consul ordered his men to take up *their* arms.
15. We are in possession of the lands taken from the enemy's *hands*.
16. He made his will openly, and appointed me his heir (*Lat.*, wrote me heir).

17. The Romans withdrew into the city.
18. His own countrymen drove Hannibal from the state.
19. No other person has the opportunity of deceiving us.
20. *When* Arion *was* cast into the sea a dolphin took *him* up.

EXERCISE LIV.

TABLE OF VERBS—Third Conjugation, *L, M, N, P* Stems.

Look out consulo ; reliquus ; inveteratus ; tantus ; concino ; decerno ; pello.

1. Genius is nourished by industry.
2. Learning is the nutriment of the human intellect [*Lat.*, The intellect of man is nourished by learning (*gerund*)].
3. Caesar seeks your advice (*Lat.*, consults you).
4. Caesar takes thought for your interest (*Lat.*, consults for you).
5. He has cheated and deceived *his* partner.
6. It only remains (*Lat.*, it is left) that I should take thought for myself.
7. You drove, with stones, men of mark out of the forum (*simple ablative*).
8. Habitual vices are eradicated with greater difficulty.
9. All with one voice lament the present position of affairs (*Lat.*, the present position of affairs is mourned with one voice of all).
10. I had rather buy than beg.
11. What overpowering compulsion was pressing *upon* you ?
12. So far from selling their corn, they even offered to buy corn (*Lat.*, Not only were they not selling corn, but even they were buying).
13. A piper cannot play without his pipes.
14. I despised the swords of Catiline.
15. Abundance of subject-matter produces abundance of words.

16. The Dictator placed in the Capitol a wreath of gold, as a gift to Jove.
17. All the parts of the universe are in harmony with each other.
18. The senate voted a triumph for Africanus.
19. *That* which moves itself never ceases to be in motion (*pass.*).
20. All on a sudden the bridge was broken down by a storm of wind and a vast rush of water (*Lat.*, force of winds and volume of water).

EXERCISE LV.

TABLE OF VERBS—Third Conjugation, *R, S, T* Stems.

Look out iugum ; condicio ; partim ; transmitto.

1. O that I could rush straightway into the arms of my *dear* Tullia !
2. No one held the consulship for more than a year.
3. Here, soldiers, where for the first time you have met the enemy, *you* must conquer or die.
4. The dog will not hurt you unless *he is* provoked.
5. Not a man uttered a word (*Lat.*, voice) in behalf of the state.
6. Many of those (*iste*) trees were planted by my own hand.
7. The Menapii sent envoys to Caesar to sue for peace.
8. Stripped of their arms and clothes they were sent under the yoke (*Lat.*, unarmed and naked).
9. Caesar has not the least intention of disbanding his army (*Lat.*, is by no means about to dismiss).
10. The opportunity of making terms has been lost (*Lat.*, the time of conditions).
11. Cadmus and Hermione were changed into snakes.
12. I will fetch my father.
13. I have for a long time been desirous of visiting Alexandria and the rest of Egypt.

14. Cratippus came to Ephesus to pay his respects to me.
15. Some of *my* friends have forsaken me, some have even betrayed *me* (*Lat.*, my friends have partly——partly).
16. I must not forsake the cause of an old friend.
17. You *are* the very man I was looking for.
18. The cranes, in search of warmer climes (*places*), cross the sea.
19. We have not provoked you, Antony, by any act of injustice.
20. Old age withdraws us from active life (*res gerere*).

EXERCISE LVI.

TABLE OF VERBS—Third Conjugation, *U, V, X* Stems and Verbs ending in *sco.*

Look out exercitatio; acuo; studium; oratio, sermo; fluo; opinio; imbuo; silentium; decerto.

1. Practice in speaking (*gen.*) makes a ready (*acuo*) tongue.
2. Your obliging disposition refuses nothing to my earnest desire.
3. The sequel (*Lat., the things* which follow) ought to agree with the commencement (*dat. pl.*).
4. One style of oratory does not suit every case.
5. All these *notions* have sprung from the same source.
6. A-belief-in-*the-existence* (*opinio*) of the gods pervades the minds of all men.
7. The crimes of parents are often expiated by the sufferings of their sons.
8. You depreciate the fame of Pompeius.
9. P. Clodius determined to harass the state.
10. He is making trouble for himself.
11. The Etrurians abandoned their camp in the stillness of night.
12. He has left no room for our entreaties or *our* warnings.

13. Conon rebuilt the walls of Athens.
14. Verres made no payment at all to the states for corn.
15. I had made up my mind to live on extremely intimate terms with him.
16. As soon as day broke (*Lat.*, when it grew light) they drew the fleet back into deep *water.*
17. Fortune has made you (*Lat.*, appointed you) a witness and a spectator of my follies.
18. To live in accordance with nature is the chief good.
19. We grow old gradually and imperceptibly (*Lat.*, gradually without feeling age grows old).
20. Pompeius at the exhortation of all his friends had arranged to risk a decisive battle (*Lat.*, to fight it out in a battle).

EXERCISE LVII.

TABLE OF VERBS—Fourth Conjugation.

Look out opus ; omitto ; imperium ; tumulus ; invenio, reperio ; fulcio ; dissentio.

1. We found the boy sitting in *his* bedchamber.
2. Antonius blockaded Mutina with siege-works and intrenchments.
3. We are anxious to prop up the state *that is* tottering and almost falling.
4. Cover *your* head.
5. I think precisely as (*Lat.*, this very thing that) I have spoken.
6. But let us say no more about oracles, let us come to dreams.
7. Navigators in doubling capes often perceive extraordinary changes of the wind (*pl.*).
8. Catiline was found far away from his *men* in the midst of the dead bodies of the enemy.

9. They cut their way through the enemy with the sword (*Lat.*, opened a way).
10. He found the rest of the ships ready for sailing, and equipped with all stores (*res*).
11. Let us draw water out of the well.
12. Our sovereignty ought to rest on renown and the good-feeling of *our* allies.
13. I have often differed from my *friend* Cato.
14. I will stay in Italy till your letter reaches me.
15. The men who had fallen in the battle (*acies*) were buried in the same tomb.
16. Rise and bury *thy* son.
17. It is a crime to put a Roman citizen in chains.
18. Verres used to keep Roman citizens in chains and in prison (*Lat.*, bound and shut up).
19. Camillus leaped on *his* horse.
20. Milo, when he had leaped down from the carriage, defended himself stoutly.

EXAMINATION PAPER L.

On Parts I. *to* IV.

1. Write in full the Subjunctive tenses Imperfect of volo, nolo, malo, eo, fio, fero.

2. What are the principal parts of aufero, affero, effero, differo, infero, suffero ?

3. What are the two chief rules for expressing *Time ?*

4. What are the Perfects of gero, lĕgo, parco, vivo, labor, orior, patior, ĕdo, ēdo, concutio, reperio?

5. Give the Genders and Genitives of opus, ordo, pulvis, tellus, pectus, quies, aer.

6. Decline felix, spes, dies, tribus, opus, lis, vulnus, stirps, supellex, caper.

7. Give the Comparatives of benevolus, primus, pulcher, and the Superlatives of niger, sacer, novus, vetus.

8. Give examples of the way of expressing Fractions in Latin.

9. Render in Latin the following phrases and sentences :—

English.	Latin.
(1) to hear good news.	to hear what we wish.
(2) every other day.	on alternate days.
(3) a pretext for revolution.	a cause of new arrangements.
(4) all to a man.	all to one.
(5) in war and peace.	in peace.
(6) to a great extent.	use *ex* and *pars.*
(7) the law of nature.	*lex.*
(8) the law of nations.	*ius.*
(9) consul for the second time.	again consul.
(10) to stay at home.	
(11) Tullia and I are well.	
(12) we hear good news daily about Dolabella.	
(13) they are seeking day and night a pretext for revolution.	
(14) I removed all suspicion.	*suffero.*
(15) I cannot but send to you.	
(16) I had much rather stay at home.	
(17) almost as many.	not many less.
(18) no harm.	nothing of evil.
(19) no man of experience.	no one learned.
(20) you tell me in your letter.	you write.

EXERCISE LVIII.—Recapitulatory.

Look out otiosus ; sexcenti ; nescio an ; opera, opes, opus ; desidia, inertia ; aveo.

1. Cato no doubt might have amused himself at Tusculum.

2. Themistocles might have enjoyed his ease.

3. One might adduce a thousand instances of that kind (*Lat.*, six hundred *instances*).

4. I cannot refrain from sending you a letter.

5. Friendship is never at a loss for opportunities (*Lat.*, has opportunities in abundance).

6. I doubt whether Gracchus had an equal in oratorical power.

7. I have not a higher opinion of any one in the world.
8. At length you may transact your own business.
9. I will do (*Lat.*, I will not neglect) all that can be done.
10. He erected almost as many statues as he took away.
11. You must undertake this work.
12. Caesar, though he (*qui*) had immense resources, was cut off by the valour of a small band (*Lat.*, a few only).
13. I took the business in hand, as I was bound to do, without any delay.
14. All with one voice agree as to the advantage of friendship.
15. They who through laziness live an idle life, still find enjoyment in degrading sloth.
16. You should help your brother.
17. You should have helped your sister.
18. You might have helped me immensely.
19. I do not like to run away ; I am eager to fight.
20. I do not like to write at greater length on this subject.

PART IV.

EXERCISE LIX.

THE ACCUSATIVE AND INFINITIVE. § 186, 187.

Look out taceo, sileo ; studium ; accido, fio ; doceo ; imprudens.

1. The young man hopes to have a long life.
2. I think that no harm has happened to Scipio.
3. Did you suppose (*pl.*) that I should say nothing (*taceo*) on matters of such importance ?
4. I hope to have very strong support from all classes (*gen.*)
5. Pansa promised to satisfy the country by *his* death or victory.
6. The Stoics tell *us* that all things happen by destiny.

7. I never felt anything more distressing than my inability to yield to the entreaties of your mother.
8. I do not intend to do that which I said I should do.
9. It was a well-known fact that Paulus was in Macedonia at that time.
10. I am glad that that matter has not disappointed your expectation.
11. It is certain that Pompeius is very friendly to us.
12. Now I perceive that she is wicked and that I am a wretched *woman*.
13. The result proved (*doceo*) that fortune assists the brave.
14. No man of experience ever said that a change of policy is fickleness.
15. You tell me in your letter that your advice is sought by Caesar.
16. He said he never had enjoyed a draught more (*Lat.*, drunk more pleasantly).
17. I see that you will be of very great use to me.
18. He was hoping to crush the enemy when off their guard.
19. I will prove that Verres took sums of money in violation of the laws.
20. I am extremely vexed that you have given up going out to dinner (*pl.*).

EXERCISE LX.

CASES WITH ADJECTIVES. § 188 to 192.

Look out monstrum ; ineo ; multitudo, populus, plebs ; religio ; sententia.

1. Macedonia is full of the enemy.
2. Pythagoras and Plato divide the soul into two parts, one partaking of reason, the other devoid *of it*.
3. Is he so ignorant of our discipline and practice ?
4. Is not this marvellous ? (*Lat.*, like a prodigy.)
5. He conceived a scheme full of crime and daring.

6. No man was ever more dear to the populace.
7. Death is common to every age.
8. Does not a dog resemble a wolf?
9. Cold is the opposite of heat.
10. Caesar selected a spot suitable for a camp.
11. You know that Marcellinus is angry with you.
12. This *course* will be highly pleasing to me, and I beg you again and again to adopt it.
13. I have no need of revenge or consolation (*pl.*).
14. At the present time I have need of your counsels, *your* affection, and *your* fidelity.
15. *His* mind was not free from religious scruples.
16. The soldiers are weary with standing.
17. A poet is akin to an orator.
18. Death is the opposite of life.
19. What need have you of our assistance?
20. I have received your letter, full of very weighty words and sentiments.

EXERCISE LXI.

CASES DEPENDING ON VERBS. § 193 to 196.

Look out evado ; annuus ; sententiam rogare ; dico, creo.

1. This man will never make a fine speaker.
2. He wished to be styled and reckoned the Father of *his* country.
3. Would that he might become a better man !
4. So far from being *thought* rich, they ought even to be considered poor.
5. Two kings were elected annually at Carthage to-hold office-for-a-year (*annuus*).
6. Pompeius gained the title of Imperator in that battle.
7. Frequently in the senate did Q. Catulus give the name of Father of *his* country to Cicero.

8. He gives to the city the name of Lavinium.
9. The city received the name of Lavinium.
10. Hannibal demanded of the magistrates the keys of the gates.
11. Racilius asked me first *for my* opinion.
12. We ask advice from you.
13. I wish to ask you one *question*.
14. He conceals nothing from us.
15. Panaetius calls Plato the Homer of philosophers.
16. You have been a bond-slave from childhood.
17. Here we shall live a life of security (*tutus*).
18. Murena was first asked *to give his* opinion.
19. Q. Servilius Ahala *was* made dictator: he named T. Quintius master of the knights.
20. Fortune instructs the vanquished too in the science of war.

EXERCISE LXII.

GENITIVE WITH VERBS. § 198 to 201.

Look out ambitus; reus; maiestas; peculatus; pecuniae repetundae; nequitia; caput.

1. P. Cornelius Sulla was condemned for bribery.
2. Cicero defended C. Sextus Roscius when on his trial for parricide.
3. He was condemned on-a-charge-of (*de*) high treason.
4. P. Sulla put Gabinius on his trial for bribery.
5. Both of them were convicted of embezzlement.
6. Cicero spoke twice in defence of C. Cornelius *when he was* accused of treason (*Lat.*, defended in two speeches).
7. A short time after *this*, Catiline, being accused of extortion, had been prevented from being a candidate for (*simple infinitive*) the consulship.
8. Memmius has prosecuted many persons for capital-offences (*capitis*), *but* he has not often spoken in defence of the accused.

9. L. Opimius was accused of high treason by Q. Decius, tribune of the plebs, on account of the death of C. Gracchus.

10. L. Manlius Torquatus pleaded in behalf of (*Lat.*, was advocate for) Catiline when he was accused of extortion.

11. It is a great work, and *one that* needs no little practice.

12. Often did your ancestors have compassion on the commons of Rome.

13. Good citizens remember the benefits *received from* their country.

14. Curio all on a sudden forgot the whole case.

15. I cannot forget your dignity.

16. I convict myself of sloth and carelessness.

17. You put me on my trial for the fault of another.

18. I want advice : you will do what may seem best to be done.

19. Catiline reminded one of *his* poverty, another of his lust.

20. Would that I had been informed of your design!

EXERCISE LXIII.

DATIVE WITH VERBS. § 202.

Look out infans ; pagina ; indulgeo ; persuadeo ; prorsus ; tueor.

1. Answerest thou me nothing ?

2. Is any one angry with little-children ?

3. Pythagoras assigns great authority to divination.

4. I will reply first to the last page of your letter (*Lat.*, your last page).

5. *My* enemies have been envious of my position (*honos*).

6. I beg you to pardon me *in* this *matter* (acc.).

7. I admit that I regarded you with favour.

8. Let us keep a command over the passions, to which the rest *of mankind* are slaves.

9. Take care of your health.
10. Sometimes I feel a little envious of you, Crassus, in this matter.
11. No injury can now be inflicted on me by those fellows.
12. I entreat you not to spare expense in any particular.
13. I fear he may give way to indignation and wrath.
14. I am satisfied of your *good* faith.
15. I never could be induced to believe that *our* souls perish at the same time as *our* bodies.
16. In the first page of my letter I reply to your last page.
17. First then I will reply to Postumus.
18. I satisfy myself that *matters* are precisely as you describe *them*.
19. In maintaining our friendship I do not favour you more than myself.
20. When Marcellus had captured the city of Syracuse, he spared all the public and private buildings.

EXAMINATION PAPER M.

On PARTS R *to* IV.

1. Decline in the Plural sus, mare, sal, locus, castra.
2. Write the Imperative Mood of partior, capio, duco, utor, eo, fero.
3. Write out in full :—

   The Perfect tenses Indicative of debeo.

   The First Person Singular of each tense in the Indicative of vivo.

   The Future Imperfect of nolo.
4. Give the Comparative of senex, frugi, felix, and the Superlative of pulcher, vetus, potius.
5. What are the principal parts of fodio, tango, cado, rideo, ardeo, audeo, domo ?
6. What are the Datives Singular of caro, domus, dos, palus, cinis, pulvis, iter, anas, puls ?

7. Write down some Unipersonal Verbs with the construction they take.

8. What Cases do the following Verbs take :—memini, egeo, noceo, libero, impero, impleo ?

9. Render in Latin the following phrases and sentences :—

English.	Latin.
(1) to adopt a sound policy.	to use good counsels.
(2) the sense of sight.	use the gerund.
(3) the sense of hearing.	use one word only.
(4) a religious obligation.	one word.
(5) to form a right judgment.	to judge rightly.
(6) profligate behaviour.	profligacy.
(7) without any public authority.	with no public counsel.
(8) in order to keep up one's position.	for the sake of dignity.
(9) this is what I want to know.	two words.
(10) I agree with you.	
(11) you bound the Roman people by a religious obligation.	*obstringĕre.*
(12) I am ashamed of your profligate conduct, though you are not ashamed of it yourself.	of which you.
(13) you do not form, in my opinion, a right judgment.	as you seem to me.
(14) to all appearance we are adopting a sound policy.	as we seem.
(15) of all the senses that of sight is the keenest.	repeat *sensus* twice.
(16) he does all this to keep up his position.	
(17) mental excitement.	excitement of mind.
(18) bodily pain.	pain of body.
(19) to run a risk.	to approach danger.
(20) nothing worth mentioning.	*admodum.*

EXERCISE LXIV.

ABLATIVE WITH VERBS. § 203 to 206.

Look out careo, egeo ; separo ; irruo.

1. Dead men are without feeling and life.

2. A wise man is free from wrathfulness.

3. I lament that the Roman people has been so long deprived of his counsel and of your voice.

4. Twice did C. Marius relieve Italy from a siege and from the dread of slavery.
5. The wall was stripped of *its* defenders.
6. A wise man is always free from every mental excitement.
7. Therefore you freed the city from danger and the state from alarm.
8. The woman has abundance of impudence.
9. Clodius is not free from suspicion in this affair.
10. The plains are filled with a confused-heap (*strages*) of men and splendid armour.
11. Not philosophers only, but our ancestors also, made a distinction between superstition and reverential feelings (*Lat.*, separated superstition from).
12. Sickness deprives me of sleep.
13. It is said that Democritus put out his own eyes.
14. Caesar ordered the soldiers to fill the trench with brushwood.
15. The sun pervades all things with his light.
16. He has robbed me of the protection of honest men.
17. I induced the father of Curio to stop him from *having* intercourse with you.
18. Brutus restrained Dolabella, *who was* hurrying to Asia, from advancing further (*Lat.*, from progress).
19. You have deprived me of great amusement and delight.
20. I hope our friendship does not need witnesses.

EXERCISE LXV.

THE ABLATIVE ABSOLUTE. § 207.

Look out vesperasco ; iumentum ; comitia ; inchoo ; Iugurthinus ; pervenio.

1. Syracuse was founded by the Corinthians under the command of Archias.

2. After the murder of Dion, Timoleon again got possession of Syracuse.
3. Metellus spoke in defence of L. Cotta when Africanus accused *him*.
4. Clodius thinks he will have kingly power, if Milo be slain.
5. When evening came on, he quenched his thirst with a draught of cold water.
6. Having received hostages, he leads back his army to the sea.
7. When the German war was finished, Caesar made up his mind that for many reasons his policy was to cross the Rhine (*gerundive*).
8. Themistocles crossed over to Asia in the reign of Artaxerxes.
9. Horatius, having slain the three Curiatii, and having lost his two brothers, returned home victorious.
10. You will look for me, if the gods be favourable (*Lat.*, help) before the winter *sets in*.
11. At length, when beasts of burden and men had been wearied to no purpose, the camp *was* pitched on the mountain ridge.
12. The Dictator, having received the consul's army from Fulvius Flaccus the lieutenant, *passed* through the Sabine country *and* reached Tibur.
13. When he knew of the arrival of Caesar, Ariovistus sent envoys to him.
14. The soldiers of Jugurtha at a given signal attack the camp of the enemy.
15. Augustus was born in the consulship of Cicero and Antonius.
16. The cowardly soldier throws away his shield and flees as fast as he can.
17. The king, having dropped the war that he had begun, returned to Ephesus.

18. When Roscius had received his directions he left Caesar and reached Capua (*Lat.*, from Caesar he reached Capua), where he found the consuls and Pompeius.
19. Sempronius at the close of the election (*Lat.*, when the election was concluded) went back to the army.
20. Caesar takes possession of the town and stations a garrison there.

EXERCISE LXVI.

PARTITIVE GENITIVE.   § 208.

Look out supplicium ; admodum ; severitas ; contendo ; spatium ;
quam minimum.

1. We have wasted much time in that single discussion.
2. There was no news in Curio's letter.
3. I hear there is neither gold nor silver in Britain.
4. We have exacted punishment enough.
5. I have plenty of employment in healing the wounds that have been inflicted on the country.
6. Curio knew nothing worth mentioning of literature.
7. Crassus with (*in*) his consummate courtesy had also a fair amount of gravity, Scaevola with all his (*in multa*) gravity was still not deficient in courtesy.
8. I have a better helper (*Lat.*, more help) in you than in him.
9. What advantage have I in deceiving you ?
10. The siege of Anticyra did not cause much delay (*Lat.*, Anticyra in besieging).
11. A father is satisfied with a small punishment for a great offence.
12. I have no confidence in Clodius.
13. To this place the Gauls pressed on with great speed, so as to give the Romans the least possible time for rallying and arming themselves. (*Turn the subordinate sentence into the passive form.*)

14. Never in any battle was there less flight or more slaughter.
15. Murena never put more work on the soldiers (*sing.*) than he took on himself.
16. There is but little reason to expect you will do this of your own will.
17. Time produces no novelties.
18. I have run risk enough.
19. He has been punished sufficiently.
20. You have inflicted punishment enough.

EXAMINATION PAPER N.

On Parts I to IV.

1. Decline seges, celer, iubar, filia, domus, vis, ego, iste, vellus, rete, grex, merx, sacer, dexter.

2. Write in Latin, 6, 16, 26, 4th, 14th, 20th.

3. What are the genders of cupido, margo, flos, carcer, pulvis, cos, dens, lis, quies ?

4. Give the principal parts of curro, suadeo, quaero, queror, veho, nascor, ulciscor, veto.

5. What Case do the following Prepositions take : ob, prae, supra, pro, sub, inter ?

6. Write the Imperative Mood of habeo, dico, aperio, nolo, memini, vereor, hortor.

7. Distinguish between cĕdo, cēdo ; dĭco, dīco ; ŏdo, ōdo ; lăbor, lābor ; lĕvis, lēvis ; mălum, mālum.

8. Render in Latin the following phrases and sentences :—

English.	Latin.
(1) to be extremely ill.	*valde* with a verb.
(2) to be highly delighted.	
(3) to my way of thinking.	as my opinion takes *me*.
(4) a city in Macedonia.	of.
(5) after the destruction of Hasdrubal's army.	past participle.
(6) sorrow for the past.	*ex.*
(7) fear for the future.	in.
(8) from a place of safety.	two words.

(9) to be reconciled to Caesar.

(10) to reconcile Pompey to Caesar. — *redigĕre.*

(11) it is reported that Pompey is very ill.

(12) words cannot express my great joy. — it cannot be expressed how.

(13) I received your letter on the 16th of February.

(14) I have no hesitation about coming to you at once.

(15) we are bound to follow the guidance of nature. — *as a* guide.

(16) you give the proper answer.

(17) ten days ago. — before these ten days.

(18) to deliver a vigorous harangue. — to speak with consummate earnestness.

(19) to gain a naval victory. — to conquer with a fleet.

(20) king of Macedon. — of the Macedonians.

EXERCISE LXVII.—Recapitulatory.

Look out succenseo, irascor ; rescribo ; reus ; pendo ; consilium ; dominor.

1. Do you say you do not know me ? I do.
2. I heard you were extremely annoyed with him.
3. Who says that these things are not useful ?
4. I will send a brief reply to your letter.
5. He ordered the man to be hanged on a wild-olive tree.
6. The mind of Otho was not effeminate, as his body was (*Lat.*, and like his body).
7. He shows himself to be worthy of his ancestors.
8. Ye need a shield more than a sword.
9. You put me on trial for the offence of another.
10. Plato asserts that no one can be a great poet without a touch of madness.
11. There is no danger.
12. I heard that Clodius had paid the penalty of his own recklessness.
13. I wish my speech to be not understood rather than censured.

14. He admits his ignorance on many points.
15. He cannot bear to be so poor.
16. Antonius said he thought you were very like me.
17. The army took an oath to Eumenes that it would pro-
    tect him and would never desert him.
18. He says he is not at home.
19. Passion is no friend to judgment.
20. All the chief virtues must needs lie dormant while
    pleasure holds supreme sway.

PART V.

EXERCISE LXVIII.

PREPOSITIONS. § 209—Ad.

Look out confugio ; invenio ; exiguus ; immolo ; contentio ; Aegates ;
Trebia.

1. I went down to the forum.
2. We flee for refuge to thee.
3. He rose to reply.
4. Caesar let back *his* army to the coast.
5. The fellow is of no use for any employment (*res*).
6. He has pleasure-grounds by the Tiber.
7. Neoptolemus gained *his* name at Troy.
8. He posted armed men at all the approaches.
9. This is no concern of mine.
10. I am sure that Mummius was at Corinth.
11. The sensation of dying lasts *but* a short time.
12. He slaughtered all the prisoners to a man.
13. I shall return to Rome by the 1st of January.
14. He will come back within ten years.
15. Whether *it* was *so, or* whether it was not, *is* nothing to
    the purpose.
16. The ships were constructed and equipped in the follow-
    ing fashion.

17. The Romans gained a naval victory over the Carthaginians in the first Punic War off the Aegates Islands.
18. Sempronius, having paid a visit to Rome after the battle at the Trebia to elect consuls, went back to the army at the close of the election.
19. Cato delivered a vigorous harangue before the people against Sergius Galba.
20. The envoys of the Helvetii flung themselves at the feet of Caesar.

EXERCISE LXIX.

PREPOSITIONS. § 209—Adversus *to* Extra.

Look out tútor (*vb.*); fines; cognitum habeo.

1. I will not strive against you.
2. I defended my frontier with arms against armed men.
3. He lived before the time of Socrates.
4. He sent the cavalry in advance (*Lat.*, before himself).
5. I never saw you before the present day.
6. I rose before daylight.
7. I saw Pompeius ten days ago.
8. He died before my consulship.
9. Sulla took the camp of the Samnites in front of the town of Nola.
10. I have acquired great influence with Pompeius.
11. I hope my entreaties will have influence with you (*pure subjunctive*).
12. He was put on his trial before the judges.
13. The name of Hannibal was very famous among the Romans.
14. The shops round the forum *were* closed.
15. Come back to this spot about noon.
16. Brutus at that time was three miles on this side of Velia.
17. He sent envoys round to the neighbouring nations.
18. About five hundred fell *on the side* of the Romans.

19. They lead an unnatural life.
20. I am fully aware of your good feeling towards me.

EXERCISE LXX.

PREPOSITIONS. § 209—In, with the Accusative.

Look out effero ; fero ; arbiter ; iudex ; distribuo ; provideo ; imploro.

1. He brought up an army to the city, or rather into the city.
2. The soldiers uplifted Otho on their shoulders.
3. This falls within our comprehension.
4. Advance the standards against the enemy.
5. Who was the umpire in respect of this business ?
6. He spoke at length (*Lat.*, many *words*) in support of that opinion.
7. Did you sit as judge in the case of Fabricius ?
8. The blood is diffused from the heart over the whole body.|
9. He asked the man to dinner for the following day.
10. On the delivery of this speech the thoughts of all were changed in an astonishing way.
11. Let me tell you (*Lat.*, know) that your honour is a subject of increasing anxiety to me day by day.
12. *A stock of* corn had not been laid in for the winter.
13. The case was brought up for trial.
14. The augur laid his right hand on the head of Numa.
15. Caesar arranged the cavalry in three divisions.
16. Hannibal divided the spoil among his men.
17. The Romans stood in battle array from sunrise till late in the day.
18. He crucified Roman citizens, appealing to the rights of freedom and citizenship.
19. The canton is divided into two parts by a river.
20. At that place Labienus had made a rampart ten feet high.

EXERCISE LXXI.

PREPOSITIONS. § 209—Infra, Inter, Intra, Iuxta.

Look out infimus; similitudo; comparo; ingredior; societas.

1. Caesar led his men to the shore below the town (*Lat.*, to the sea).
2. I hold you to be lower than the lowest of mankind.
3. He considers human affairs beneath his notice (*Lat.*, placed beneath him).
4. Friendship cannot exist except between the virtuous.
5. The consuls divided the armies between them.
6. The boys have a striking likeness to one another.
7. It is very disgraceful to compare these *things* one with the other.
8. The consul had been brought back among many *who were* wounded.
9. They were overwhelmed while considering whether to flee or to fight (*Lat.*, between the plan of flight and battle).
10. A free state and a king are naturally opposed to each other.
11. The towns are not more than half a mile apart.
12. These *notions* are inconsistent with each other.
13. He will die within twenty days.
14. Meanwhile the horsemen had been already sent forward to Alba.
15. The Belgae prevented the Cimbri from setting foot within their borders.
16. A league was formed between Philip king of Macedon and Hannibal.
17. Let us keep our quarrels to ourselves (*Lat.*, carry on between ourselves).
18. The boys love one another.
19. Strange *was* the difference between the army and the Emperor.

20. For fourteen years they had not entered a house (*Lat.*, gone under a roof).

EXERCISE LXXII.

PREPOSITIONS. § 209—Ob, Penes, Per.

Look out talentum ; colo ; oratio ; obviam ; indutiae ; nefarius.

1. We are going to fight for *our* native land.
2. He received a talent for a single play.
3. It is for that very reason that Erechtheus is worshipped at Athens.
4. We have sent to Athens to meet Brutus.
5. The whole state had gone out to meet him as he approached the city.
6. The decision of the matter rests with you.
7. That which he acquired by crime, he squanders and wastes in debauchery.
8. An arrangement made (*Lat.*, *Quod actum est*) under compulsion ought not to be ratified.
9. He lost his life in a very disgraceful way (*Lat.*, through consummate disgrace).
10. You are so cowardly that you cannot endure the sound of a trumpet (*Lat.*, Through cowardice).
11. Brutus in writing clears Caesar from-complicity-in (*de*) the murder of Marcellus.
12. You are old enough to be his father (*Lat.*, By age he may be in the place of a son to you).
13. We are deceived by a truce and the hope of peace.
14. By a blunder he incurred most serious loss (*Lat.*, rushed into the greatest loss).
15. All dishonesty (*neut. pl.*) must be avoided for its own sake.
16. Under pretence of friendship you have betrayed me infamously.

S.L.E.]

17. Vestorius has informed me by letter that you delayed your departure from Rome because you were not very well.
18. Why do you not allow these men to enjoy their freedom?
19. On the following day a truce was made, and permission to bury the slain was granted (*Lat.*, by means of a truce).
20. In a set speech we often make rhymes by carelessness (*Lat.*, speak verses).

EXERCISE LXXIII.

PREPOSITIONS.   § 209—Post, Praeter, Prope, Propter.

Look out abdico ; receptus ; aerarium, fiscus ; consularis ; quisquam ; temere ; immineo ; iudicium.

1. Aegina was behind me, Megara in front of me.
2. Ariovistus concealed himself behind the mountain.
3. After the death of their colleague all the censors resigned office.
4. After sunset the signal for retreat was given.
5. Mine *was* the only (*unus*) house *that* the senate since the foundation (*constituere*) of this city has deemed worthy of being built at the public expense (*Lat.*, from the treasury).
6. I see you have not a single friend among (*ex*) the men of consular rank except Lucullus.
7. No one but myself holds this opinion (use *videtur*).
8. The Alban lake had swollen in an unusual degree.
9. He engages in nothing but his own business.
10. Dionysius paid me an unexpected visit.
11. No one knows the faults of a house except the owner.
12. Every one, save those engaged in trade (*Lat.*, traders), hesitates to visit Britain without a good reason (*Lat.*, does not approach recklessly).

13. Lentulus, contrary to his usual custom, had been up the whole of last night (*Lat., vigilare*, with ablative).

14. The ladies of our family (*Lat.,* our women) remained at Rome as well as the rest *of the women.*

15. How I wish you could live not only in my neighbourhood, but actually with me !

16. I wish I had come nearer to you.

17. The whole state is in alarm on account of you alone.

18. Aegina, by reason of its being so near (*Lat.,* nearness), threatened the Piraeus too much.

19. Pompey's men being alarmed retire from the camp to the town (*Lat.,* through fear).

20. When this man was praetor, fellows, whose guilt was most evident (*Lat.,* most guilty), were through bribes acquitted by the court.

EXAMINATION PAPER O.

On PART I *to* IV.

1. Decline puer, aetas, comes, tenax, alacer, ego.

2. Give the principal parts of mano, iuvo, foveo, mordeo, acio, pono, illucesco, reor, memini.

3. Write the Present Imperfect Indicative of prosum, adeo, rolo, fero, partior, utor.

4. Write in full the Imperatives of edo, memini, facio.

5. Classify the Latin Conjunctions, with examples of their ise.

6. Explain, with examples, the meaning of the terms *Deponent, Reciprocal, Intransitive, Reflexive.*

7. Write in Latin 7, 17, 207 ; 5th, 19th, 41st ; two-thirds, our-fifths.

8. What Cases do the following Verbs and Adjectives take ? —parco, credo, careo, circumdo, damno, obliviscor, memor, ptus, plenus.

9. Render in Latin the following phrases and sentences :—

ENGLISH.	LATIN.
(1) a very painstaking man.	*summus.*
(2) a man of stainless honour.	*summus.*
(3) a man with a very high sense of honour.	superlative of *pudens*
(4) the name Cato.	genitive.
(5) the word pleasure.	genitive.
(6) at the age of 30.	
(7) a fleet of 300 ships.	
(8) two notable events.	
(9) as soon as possible.	
(10) as far as you can.	futuro.
(11) Do you say you do not know me ?	three words.
(12) Who says that these things are not expedient ?	
(13) You will say, " What is that to me ?"	
(14) He says the present state of things is intolerable.	three words.
(15) People have a high opinion of you.	
(16) I fear you have not received my letter.	
(17) I have no fear about your merit satisfying the opinion men have of it.	answering the opinion of men.
(18) He resigned office.	
(19) the best authorities.	the authority of the wisest.
(20) You are not the man.	it is not yours.

EXERCISES LXXIV.

PREPOSITIONS.   § 209—Secundum, Sub, Super.

Look out concremo ; afflicio ; traduco ; praedor ; iactura, damnum, fraus.

1. He received a wound close to his ear.
2. Next to the gods, men confer the greatest benefits on their fellow-men (*Lat.*, chiefly benefit).
3. Next to you, I have no better friend than solitude (*use the neuter of* amicus).
4. Towards evening Caesar ordered the gates to be closed.

5. They burnt *their* houses over their own heads (*Lat.*, themselves).
6. They were slaughtered one after another.
7. Famine as well as disease attacked the Carthaginian army.
8. At that very time I was on the other side of the sea.
9. He slew more than two hundred thousand of the enemy; he took more than fifty thousand *prisoners*.
10. Towards night Pompeius weighed anchor.
11. Towards the end of the cavalry fight an infantry battle commenced.
12. The Gauls on account of superabundance of population and scarcity of land used to send colonies over the Rhine.
13. Having made these arrangements, he determined to build a bridge a little way above the place where he had previously taken his army across.
14. At the commencement of the civil war, when you were going towards Brundisium to Caesar, you paid me a visit at my Formian villa (*Formianum*).
15. When Pompey had pitched his camp on the other side of the river Apsus, he collected all his forces there (*eo*).
16. The Etrurians sent colonies over the Apennines.
17. This vast body (*tantum*) of the enemy is not only within the walls, but in the citadel over the forum and tho senate-house.
18. This is in accordance with nature, that no one should act in such a way as to make unfair profit from another man's ignorance.
19. A new grief was added to the old *sorrow* by the loss of so many citizens.
20. Right reason must be deemed *to be* beyond the reach of man, and must be assigned to God.

PREPOSITIONS. § 210—A, Coram, Cum.

Look out öpis ; nihilo ; firmus ; tiro ; fides.

1. We seek assistance from you.
2. Be on your guard against poison.
3. A deserter from Pyrrhus came to the camp of Fabricius.
4. The city of Rome was taken by the Gauls.
5. This is not a whit more in favour of *our* opponents than of ourselves.
6. In the west we have both leaders and armies on whom we can depend (*firmus*).
7. It was said that Antonius was strong (*firmus*) in respect of cavalry.
8. Antonius is kept in check (*Lat.*, held) on the rear, in front, *and* on the flanks.
9. I spoke to you (*Lat.*, with you) in the presence of P. Cuspius.
10. Man has then a resemblance to God.
11. You, veteran soldiers, will fight against an army of raw recruits (*exercitus tiro*).
12. The sanctity of an oath must often be kept with an enemy.
13. You too were caught with a blood-stained sword *in your hand*.
14. At the earliest dawn he came to the house of Pomponius.
15. Lentulus the consul sides with Caesar.
16. The best authorities support our view.
17. We wish to receive a reply in the presence of the Romans.
18. We are debarred by business (*pl.*) from every *kind of* amusement.

19. M. Crassus had little learning and less wit (*Lat.*, was moderately instructed by learning, *and* even more narrowly by nature).

20. I spent six months in the company of Antiochus the philosopher.

EXERCISE LXXVI.

PREPOSITIONS. § 210—De, Ex, In.

Look out occultus ; dirigo ; improvisus ; sententia ; pendeo, pendo ; interitus ; cognatus.

1. The praetor rose from his feet.
2. Lucretius and Attius cast themselves down from the wall.
3. What will become of my dear Tullia ? (*use the diminutive* Tulliola).
4. He drew off the ring from *his* finger.
5. Milo during the night returned to the city.
6. I will seek precedents for my actions from men of the highest character.
7. The rivers are swollen with the snows.
8. I will arouse you from sleep.
9. Truth lurks hidden (*Lat.*, in a hidden *place*).
10. He injures some that he may be bountiful to others.
11. These *deeds* were done openly in the forum at Syracuse before the face and in the sight of all men.
12. The Spaniards thought it better to be conquered in Spain than to be dragged as conquerors into Italy.
13. The country depends on Brutus.
14. The report of the death of Clodius has traversed the boundaries of the Roman dominion.
15. While I was making my way to Mutina I heard on the road of the battle having been fought (*factus*).
16. You purposely inflicted an injury on me.

17. Caesar came there unexpectedly, and sooner than any one thought he could come (*Lat.*, quicker than the opinion of all).
18. By the advice of friends and relations Roscius fled for refuge to Rome.
19. You are not the man to deserve well of the state.
20. What have I planned, what have I managed, what have I performed save by the advice, the authority, and the vote of this order?

EXERCISE LXXVII.

PREPOSITIONS. § 210—**Prae, Pro, Simul, Sub, Super.**

Look out maeror, luctus ; locus ; perdisco ; furtum ; consido ; ditio.

1. I cannot speak for grief.
2. I was so anxious that I could not make-jests (*Lat.*, for anxiety).
3. My tears prevent me from dwelling at further length on this topic (*Lat.*, for weeping I cannot dwell).
4. You will not see the sun through the vast number of darts and arrows.
5. In this case the consul, compared with me, will be even of less importance than a private person (*Lat.*, even less than).
6. Are you not willing to die for your friend?
7. Give an absolute denial to (*Lat.*, deny for certain) all things that are not certain.
8. We have trustworthy information about the arrival of Caesar.
9. He sets no store on wealth (*Lat.*, he regards wealth as of no account).
10. When they have no hope of mastering *a subject* they give up the desire to learn *it* (*Lat.*, they cast away the desire of learning together with the hope, etc.).

11. No slight deception lurks beneath this remark.

12. I will write to you on this subject from Rhegium.

13. We are at your command (*Lat.*, under your sway).

14. I beg you to listen favourably to me when I speak on my own behalf.

15. Caesar took his seat within the intrenchments (*sing.*) in front of the camp.

16. The affair was now not far from a mutiny.

17. The vast-throng (*multitudo*) was not far from being destitute (*Lat.*, destitution) of all necessaries (*res*).

18. I fear that I have made too small a return to you for that which I have *received* from you.

19. Sulla ordered a reward to be assigned to the poet, on condition that he did not write anything afterwards.

20. These arguments were used against and for the statute (*Lat.*, These *words* were spoken).

EXAMINATION PAPER P.

On PARTS I. *to* IV.

1. What is usually the Gender of Latin nouns denoting (*a*) trees, (*b*) mountains, (*c*) rivers, (*d*) winds? Quote exceptions to the general rules.

2. Give the Genitive Cases of gener, cancer, asper, faber, integer, sinister, dexter.

3. What are the principal parts of obliviscor, sterno, motior, soleo, haereo, gaudeo, vinco, amplector?

4. Classify the Latin Adverbs, with examples?

5. What Cases go with placeo, egeo, arguo, credo, fretus, par, utilis, conscius?

6. Compare fortiter, acriter, valde, diu, prope, ultra, bene, male.

7. Mention some Adjectives that have no degrees of comparison.

8. Write in full the Future Imperfects of possum, volo, malo, eo, fero, largior, loquor, fateor.

9. Render in Latin the following phrases and sentences :—

ENGLISH.	LATIN.
(1) a long time before.	two words.
(2) a long time after.	two words.
(3) by our own fault.	insert *ipsorum.*
(4) many important matters.	insert *et.*
(5) to do what is right.	two words.
(6) to exhort earnestly.	use *opus.*
(7) by my own fault.	insert *ipsius.*
(8) to remain in Rome.	
(9) to remain in the city.	
(10) to return to Rome.	
(11) I was compelled to do this.	*necesse.*
(12) Man must needs die.	*necesse.*
(13) We should guard against the love of glory.	*cupiditas.*
(14) Love of wealth should be avoided.	
(15) Must we not all die?	
(16) He is his own enemy.	
(17) I will not give up my rights.	yield from my right.
(18) I have such an opinion of your wisdom that . . .	I deem you a man of that wisdom.
(19) The first duty is . . .	nothing should be done before.
(20) by natural instinct.	with nature as guide.

EXERCISE LXXVIII.—Recapitulatory.

Look out excusatio; dolor; interior; evado; res familliaris; iste; clades.

1. Preparations were being made at Rome for a war with the Rutuli with great vigour.

2. You must apologise to those whom you offend unwittingly.

3. These men, by reason of their worth, were not only highly esteemed by Caesar, but were also regarded with affection by the army.

4. I wish gratitude for a kindness to have more influence with me than resentment for a wrong.

5. To say nothing of right (*Lat.*, authority), I have might too to keep you in check.

6. Who does not know that Publius Clodius was slain by the slaves of Milo on the Appian road ?

7. You ought long ago to have been led to execution (*Lat.*, death).

8. With whom does the decision rest ?

9. Perseus retired into the heart of *his* kingdom.

10. I shall return to Rome by the 15th of March.

11. I have made out nothing about this affair.

12. I have a thorough insight into the intention of Clodius.

13. Just as the enemy were on the point of scaling the wall . . .

14. I have read Xenophon's treatise on domestic economy.

15. I still hold this opinion.

16. I was two years in the province.

17. One cast himself from the wall, the other was caught and flogged to death.

18. What have I to do with such contemptible triflers ?

19. M. Cicero was born in the consulship of Q. Caepio and Q. Serranus, on the 3d of January.

20. What ? Did not C. Flaminius, in his second consulship, in the Second Punic War, set at nought warnings of what was to happen, with disastrous results to the state ?

PART VI.

EXERCISE LXXIX.

FINAL CONJUNCTIONS. § 213, 214.

Look out adipiscor ; amans ; coniunctio ; collum, cervix ; excipio ; oppugno.

1. Alcibiades required that two colleagues should be assigned to him.

2. Take heed lest you fall into the hands of *your* enemies.

3. No doubt should be entertained as to the existence of poets before Homer.

4. Do not hesitate to intrust this man with the sole charge of affairs (*Lat.*, trust all things to this one man).

5. Let me now understand your opinion (*Lat.*, what you think).

6. I did not fear that any one would lament the death of worthless citizens.

7. I never expected to come as a suppliant to you.

8. Mithridates charged the guards of the bridge not to let slip the opportunity offered by fortune for giving freedom to Greece.

9. All men desire to reach old age, and *when they have* reached *it they* find fault *with* it (*idem*).

10. I could not bring my mind to behold my brother, who loved me so dearly (*Lat.*, very fond of me), in such deep sorrow.

11. We call gods and men to witness that we took up arms not against our country, nor that we might put others in danger, but that our own persons might be protected from injustice.

12. I never did let an opportunity pass of doing my best to detach Pompeius from a close connexion with Caesar.

13. In spite of his reluctance (*Lat.*, hesitating) the soldiers had induced Cassius to risk a battle (*Lat.*, try the fortune of an engagement).

14. Caesar, fearing that the enemy might attempt to entice our men to unfavourable ground, slackens his pace (*Lat.*, proceeds more slowly).

15. Dionysius, that he might not intrust his neck to a barber, had his daughters taught to shave (*Lat.*, taught his daughters).

16. Not a man among the enemy could leave the line of march without being cut off by Caesar's cavalry.

17. Caesar required permission to send envoys to Pompeius without risk.
18. Caesar exhorted his men to avail themselves (*Lat.* use) of the favours of fortune and to storm the camp.
19. Having said this he took an oath that he would not return to the camp unless he were victorious, and he exhorted the rest to follow his example (*Lat.*, do the same).
20. It is reported that A. Cluentius bribed the court to condemn the innocent Statius Albius, with whom he was at enmity (*Lat.*, his foe).

EXERCISE LXXX.

CONSECUTIVE CONJUNCTIONS. § 215.

Look out parum abfuit ; humilis ; pungo ; perdo ; spiritus ; concursus ; adimo.

1. I cannot help sending to you.
2. It cannot be denied that it is more disgraceful to deceive than to be deceived.
3. I considered it my first duty to congratulate you.
4. He was very near being killed.
5. There was great fear at Rome lest the Gauls should again get possession of the city.
6. We are not stupid enough to make such assertions.
7. I have such an opinion of your wisdom that I do not prefer my plan to yours.
8. They fought in such a way that on neither side could the fight have been more fiercely contested.
9. Cato departed from life in such a way that he rejoiced in having found a motive for dying.
10. Many have made no account of their own lives (*sing.*) to rescue those who were dearer to them than they were to themselves.

11. I am not so uninformed and ignorant of your feelings (*sing.*) as not to know what you (*pl.*) think about the death of P. Clodius.
12. Verres all on a sudden became so crestfallen that it appeared not only to the Roman people, but even to *the man* himself, that he was convicted.
13. In the first place that letter annoyed me so much that it took away my sleep.
14. There was no doubt that one of the consuls would carry on the war against the Aequi.
15. Verres for the space of three years harassed and harried Sicily in such a way that it could by no means be restored to its old condition.
16. I did not flatter the fortune of another so far as to be dissatisfied with my own.
17. Pythagoras and Plato speak in praise of death, but with this restriction, that they forbid *us* to flee from life.
18. By these events the Pompeians gained so much fresh confidence and enthusiasm, that they did not think of the plan of the campaign, but thought they were already victors.
19. Just sufficient space was left between the two armies for the troops on each side to run to meet their foes.
20. We hope the business will ultimately turn out well.

EXERCISE LXXXI.

CAUSAL CONJUNCTIONS.　§ 216.

Look out includo ; religio ; praestans ; libertus, patronus ; inducio ; miseriae.

1. I congratulate you on having such influence with Caesar.
2. He did well to depart.
3. You acted properly in confining me within my house.

4. The cause of my journey was that I had not a place where I could be any longer in a state of independence (*pro meo iure*).

5. I could not induce the Athenians to grant a place of interment within the city; for they said they were prevented by religious scruples.

6. It is said that Theophrastus on his deathbed found fault with nature for having assigned to men so short a life.

7. A trunk was given to the elephant, because by reason of the vast size of its body it had difficulty in getting at its food (*Lat.*, difficult approaches to).

8. O that I may see the day when I can thank you for having forced me to remain alive!

9. Hannibal believed Scipio to be a man of mark, from the very fact that he had been chosen in preference to all others as a leader against him.

10. Homer represents Jupiter as complaining that he was unable to rescue, against the-will-of-destiny (*Lat.*, fate), his son Sarpedon from death.

11. Agesilaus was recalled by his countrymen, because the Boeotians and Athenians had declared war against the Lacedaemonians.

12. I was not deterred (*Lat.*, that circumstance did not deter me) from sending you a letter, by reason that you had not sent one to me, but because in such great troubles I could find nothing to write about.

13. Do you blame *him* because as a freedman he assisted his patron, who at that time was in distress?

14. I thank you, inasmuch as my letter had so much influence *with you*.

15. Was not Aristides banished from his country, because he was immoderately just?

16. Therefore it is never expedient to do wrong, because it is always disgraceful : and because it is always right, it is always expedient to be an honest man.

17. Since you will have it so, I will admit that I was too grateful.

18. You are angry with me for defending the man whom you accuse.

19. Ye accuse Sex. Roscius. On what grounds ? (*Lat.*, Why so ?) Because he escaped from your hands ; because he did not submit to be slain.

20. Inasmuch as you have desired to be made acquainted with my views and opinions (*sing.*) I will hide nothing *from you* (*Lat.*, to be partakers of).

EXAMINATION PAPER **Q.**

On PARTS I. *to* IV.

1. What classes of nouns in Latin usually have no Plural, and what no Singular ? Show the different meanings the following nouns have in the Singular and the Plural, viz., aedes, auxilium, carcer, copia, comitium, littera.

2. How many Participles has the Latin Verb in each voice ? Give examples.

3. Decline lapis, fur, later, pater, ater, remex, hiemps.

4. What Cases go with noceo, patiens, dives, gratus, similis, expers, ignosco, memini ?

5. Compare ater, vetus, utilis, senex, munificus, frugi, potis.

6. Name some of the Verbs that take *two* accusatives.

7. What is the construction of licet, miseret, oportet, pudet, libet, paenitet ?

8. How is the Perfect formed in the compounds of lĕgo, ago, claudo, cado, rego, capio, facio ?

9. Render in Latin the following phrases and sentences :—

ENGLISH.	LATIN.
(1) not strictly true.	*minus.*
(2) not absolutely essential.	*minus.*
(3) to live in the country.	

ENGLISH.	LATIN.
(4) I know not what to say.	*habeo.*
(5) I hope the matter will turn out well.	*fore ut.*
(6) I have quite a different opinion.	use *alius* and *meus.*
(7) I am inclined to think.	*in ea opinione ut.*
(8) It is my intention.	I have it in *my* mind.
(9) in that year also.	in the same year.
(10) What would you have more?	
(11) No one pities me.	
(12) They tried to deprive all of us of life.	
(13) There is no danger.	*nihil.*
(14) I expect to be in Athens in September.	
(15) After the conclusion of the war with the Sabines, Tarquin returned in triumph to Rome.	
(16) The stream was about three feet in depth.	
(17) What was I to do?	
(18) He was fighting on horseback.	from a horse.
(19) They were fighting on horseback.	from horses.
(20) We have received information.	It has been announced to us.

EXERCISE LXXXII.

TEMPORAL CONJUNCTIONS. § 217.

Look out fatigo ; patria ; arctus ; gaudeo ; obsaepio ; miser.

1. Trust me, you are surrendering the citadel (*urbem*) of philosophy, while you defend the outworks (*castella*).

2. The Sulmonenses, as soon as they saw our standards, opened their gates.

3. Before I could say (*facere*) a word, he rose from his seat and departed.

4. I will carry on the *work* I have undertaken as long as I have the power.

5. When Pherecydes saw some water that had been drawn from a well, he foretold an earthquake.

6. But nothing distressed *them* so much as thirst, inasmuch as a vast crowd of combatants and non-combatants had only one spring left for use (*Lat.*, used one remaining spring).

7. I will not cease to make entreaty until (*quoad*) we have received information that you have done that which we are looking for with great longing (*Lat.*, it has been announced to us).

8. A Roman citizen was flogged to death in the middle of the forum at Messana ; and all the while not a sound was heard from the poor victim (*gen.*) but this, "I am a Roman citizen."

9. When Conon heard that his native city was besieged, he did not inquire where he might dwell in safety, but whence he might furnish protection to his countrymen.

10. After a prolonged struggle, our men got possession of the baggage and the camp.

11. Afterwards, when we went to bed, I slept more soundly than usual (*Lat.*, a sleep more close than was wont embraced me).

12. No sooner is the creature born than it revels in enjoyment.

13. When I have seen Caesar I will proceed to Arpinum.

14. When the Gauls saw that the Romans had suddenly come down, they too, eager for the fray, rush into battle, and the fight began before the signal was given by the leaders.

15. Tarquinius arrived a little before sunset.

16. What *can be* more delightful to me than, when I cannot speak with you in person, either to write to you or to read your letters ?

17. Since I left the city, I have never let a day intervene without posting something *in the shape* of a letter to you.

18. While our men were collecting these things, the king himself escaped from their hands.
19. It is a saying, " While there is life in a sick man there is hope."
20. Before daylight surprises *us*, and larger bands of the enemy block up our path, let us sally forth.

EXERCISE LXXXIII.

CONCESSIVE AND COMPARATIVE CONJUNCTIONS.
§ 218, 219.

Look out fremo ; decedo ; turpis, honestus ; desidero ; paries, murus, moenia.

1. I do not laugh at these matters though you may.
2. Though all murmur, I will say what I think.
3. Though the Roman people was never *vanquished* in any war, still it has been beaten in many battles.
4. Though men formed societies by natural instinct, yet it was with the hope of guarding (*custodia*) their property that they sought the protection (*pl.*) of cities.
5. Here we must make a stand, comrades, as though we were fighting in front of the walls of Rome.
6. I keep up harmony as well as I can.
7. Nicias, as is his bounden duty, loves you.
8. May my prayers have an influence with you, like that which they have had in your behalf this day.
9. As all lands that are cultivated are not productive, so all minds that are tilled do not bear fruit.
10. The Romans, weary as they were, still press forward.
11. Go on as you have begun.
12. They lie just as if they were entirely without life (*animus*).
13. I indeed am just as much a slave as you are, though at home I was a freeman.

14. Though I ought to have the mastery (*perf. vinco*), still I will give up my rights.
15. That which is wrong, though it be concealed, can by no means be made right.
16. Good men do what is straightforward, what is right, though they see no prospect of gain (*Lat.*, that no gain will follow).
17. However laughable that conduct (*neut. pl. ille*) might be, as indeed it was, still it did not make me laugh.
18. I love Pomponius Atticus like a second brother.
19. And that you may not be in ignorance of that which I failed to find in your letters, I will write frankly, as my disposition and our friendship demand (*sing.*).
20. Though many may strive with me in this matter, still I shall easily master all of them.

EXERCISE LXXXIV.

CONDITIONAL CONJUNCTIONS. § 221.

Look out addo ; peto ; numne ; herus ; pactio.

1. If you wish to know, I will tell *you*.
2. If you are wise you will say nothing.
3. If I dared, I would make-for Athens.
4. I, if I have the power, will satisfy you.
5. Supposing that I learn anything fresh to-day, you shall know *it*.
6. If I receive the letter that I am expecting, I will betake myself to you.
7. If there is to be a war, I have made up my mind to be on the side of Pompeius.
8. Had you not departed from Rome before, you certainly would leave it now.
9. I shall be very grateful if you carry out your declared intention (*Lat.*, that which you declare).

10. If Hamilcar were alive, we should now be at war with the Romans.
11. I would speak at greater length, Quirites, if words could infuse courage in cowards.
12. We shall be glad if our wish is realised.
13. If you have any news of Dolabella, you will inform me.
14. Had he been a man he would never have assailed the life of a man so savagely.
15. Do you mean to tell me that if Coriolanus had friends, they were bound to take up arms with Coriolanus against their country !
16. No doubt severity must be employed by masters against their servants, if they cannot be kept in order in any other way.
17. If you are in better health by this time, I am very glad.
18. If the son of Scipio had been a healthy man, he would have been reckoned an orator (*disertus*) of the first rank.
19. Assuming that Pompeius remains in Italy and that the dispute is not settled by arrangement (*Lat.*, comes to an agreement), I think the war will be prolonged.
20. Had you addressed to yourself these words (*Lat.*, these two words), "What am I doing ?" you would not have come into that disgraceful position.

EXAMINATION PAPER R.

On Parts I. to IV.

1. Decline liber (the adjective), origo, direptio, effigies, solus, avis, pater, nox, trabs, niger, asper.
2. Give the chief parts of lavo, audeo, spargo, posco, morior, experior, expergiscor, utor.
3. Describe the main uses of the Gerund and Gerundive in Latin.
4. What are the Genitives Plural of domus, imber, mater, mare, voluptas, mas, falx ?

5. When is the Supine in *um* used, and when the Supine in *u*?

6. Write the First Person in each tense, Indicative and Subjunctive, of volo, nolo, malo, eo.

7. When is *se* used for *eum* in Latin sentences?

8. Write eight Verbs which are followed by an Accusative and Infinitive as their object.

9. Render in Latin the following phrases and sentences :—

ENGLISH.	LATIN.
(1) with the exception of your-self.	
(2) I am persuaded.	
(3) to rely on my own judgment.	*stare.*
(4) to form plans.	enter into.
(5) to turn into ridicule.	to have as a laughing-stock.
(6) to be cast in a suit.	to fall in a cause.
(7) in my judgment.	
(8) I say this unwillingly.	
(9) to detest the name Cassius.	
(10) constitutionally nervous.	by nature.
(11) Your letter gives me some relief.	*nonnihil.*
(12) He has been living at Rome for many years.	
(13) Do I not recognise your voice?	
(14) He said he would come.	
(15) The freedom of the Roman people is at stake.	
(16) I am justified in saying this.	by my *own* right.
(17) I will protect you from wrong.	ward off wrong from you.
(18) follow this example.	imitate these things.
(19) the opinion you profess (*pl.*).	carry before you.
(20) to hold fast an opinion.	persevere in.

EXERCISE LXXXV.

THE RELATIVE. § 222 to 228.

Look out imperium ; anima ; civilis ; dissensio ; ira, iracundia ; persevero ; perfero ; sono, cano.

1. I have read the letter that Brutus sent you from Asia.

2. I will not deceive your opinion of my honesty.

3. Coriolanus acted impiously in that he sought aid from the Volscians.

4. No man can speak to the purpose save *one* who has a sound knowledge *of his subject*.

5. Many months before he stated in the senate that he intended to act as he has acted.

6. It was a favourite saying of Thrasea, "He that hates vices hates men" (*Lat.*, Thrasea used frequently to say).

7. But we seek not sovereignty nor wealth, for the sake of which all wars and contests among men occur (*Lat.*, are), but freedom, which no good man loses without *losing* his life at the same time.

8. I do not intend to speak of the views of those who give the name of surrender to an odious slavery, nor do I think that these men are to be regarded as citizens or called upon for advice.

9. What is it, Catiline? Do you hesitate to do at my bidding that which you were already doing of your own free will?

10. Call to mind, Quirites, all the disturbances in the state, not only those of which you have heard, but those which you yourselves remember and *which* you saw *with your own eyes*.

11. The man who does not protect his *friends* from wrong, when he has the power, acts unjustly.

12. Two opinions have been expressed, but I do not approve either.

13. What can be more unfair than this—that we should be coming to a decision about peace without the knowledge of those who are conducting the war? and not only without their knowledge, but even against their will?

14. Follow this example (*Lat.*, imitate these *things*), ye who seek honour, praise, *and* fame (repeat *qui*).

15. The same enthusiasm, which had carried the Romans through the midst of the enemy's host, also carried them right into the camp.
16. Caesar, having accomplished his purpose (*Lat.*, that which he had proposed in *his* mind), ordered the signal for retreat to be sounded.
17. Pythagoras was in Italy in the days when L. Brutus made his country free.
18. All that remains, Quirites, is that you should hold fast the opinion that you profess.
19. Some there are who through dread of odium dare not express their views (*Lat.*, what they think), excellent though they may be.
20. Nothing that is devoid of justice can be right.

EXERCISE LXXXVI.

THE RELATIVE—*continued.* § 222 to 228.

Look out saeculum ; existo ; conubium ; pecco ; tego.

1. This shall be the post for you to occupy (*subj.*).
2. The husbandman plants trees, which are to benefit another generation.
3. Do you not yet see clearly by whose agency, by whose machinations, by whose crime we were ruined ?
4. There are (*existo*) many things in the body which sharpen (*subj.*) the intellect, and many which blunt it.
5. The soldiers for the most part made their way to the forum, with the desire to see the spot on which Galba had fallen.
6. Then Romulus by the advice of the fathers sent envoys to the neighbouring states around to solicit friendship and intermarriage with the new people.
7. Your age is such that it has already escaped from the passionate desires of youth.

8. I do not think you are the sort of man to think that the Cyclopes fashioned the thunderbolt for Jove on Aetna.

9. I sent the brave C. Sulpicius, the praetor, to take out of the house of Cethegus any weapons that might be there.

10. Two Roman knights were found to relieve you from that anxiety and to undertake to murder me in my own bed (*lectulus*) on that very night shortly before the break of day.

11. He was a fool to give me this silver.

12. You do not deserve to have vessels of such fine workmanship; they are suitable to my rank (*sum*, with genitive).

13. Who is there at the present day whose interest it is that that statute should be in force (*Lat.*, remain)?

14. You are the only person, C. Caesar, in whose victory no man has fallen unless he had arms in his hands (*Lat.*, armed).

15. Who could be friendly to Domitius and *at the same time* (*qui*) on bad terms with you?

16. Who ever held a province with an army and yet never sent a single despatch to the senate?

17. I am not yet speaking of what you did, but of what you allowed to be done.

18. I seem to have done wrong in departing from you.

19. I wish you would write me word as to the day on which you expect to leave Rome.

20. We have concealed our opinion (*Lat.*, what we thought) too long.

EXERCISE LXXXVII.

THE RELATIVE—*continued.* § 222 to 228.

Look out peto ; ultro ; indico ; invidia ; probus ; dego ; concido ; opprimo ; requiro ; flagitium ; confero.

1. A young man hopes that he will have a long life, but this is a thing that an old man cannot expect.

2. There were some who believed that Crassus was not ignorant of the design.

3. Julius Naso is a candidate for public-office (*pl.*); he has many strong competitors (*Lat.*, he is a candidate with many, with good *men*), and, as it is creditable, so it is hard to beat them.

4. Timoleon, when he was advanced in life, lost his eye-sight, but not from any disease; yet he endured that misfortune with such calmness that no one heard him complain, nor did he for that reason take less part in private and public business.

5. It is more easy to find men who will devote themselves spontaneously to death than men who can endure pain with resignation.

6. For there are and have been philosophers holding that the gods take no thought at all for the affairs of men.

7. There are some who think that death consists in a departure of the soul from the body.

8. Great is the power of conscience, and they who neglect it, when they wish to wrong me, will betray themselves.

9. You have a consul, who will not hesitate to obey your decrees, and to defend, as long as he lives, the ordinances that you have made.

10. You will look in vain hereafter for a citizen, who will expose himself to odium to save his country.

11. That father must be a virtuous man, who requires his son to be more virtuous than he himself has been.

12. Never then can praise equal to her deserts (*satis digne*) be bestowed on philosophy; for if a man follow her *dictates* he may pass his whole life free from vexation.

13. There are, however, other philosophers, ay, great and famous men (*Lat.*, and these indeed great, etc.), who

hold that the whole universe is governed and regulated by the intellect and reason of the gods.

14. Such, M. Antonius, were my plans for *the welfare of* the state, and had they prevailed the state would now be standing ; you would have fallen under the weight (use *concidĕre*) of your crimes, *your* poverty, and your degradation.

15. Pompeius, fearing an ambuscade, I suppose, because these events had turned out contrary to his expectation (for he had seen his own men a little while before fleeing from their camp), did not venture to approach the intrenchments for a considerable time.

16. The next day Domitius drew near to Nicopolis, and pitched his camp close to the town (use *conferre*) ; and while our men were fortifying this camp, Pharnaces drew up his troops in his own peculiar fashion (*Lat.*, in his own custom and arrangement).

17. I commend to your *notice* my very intimate friend, T. Pinarius, with an earnestness that I cannot increase (*Lat.*, with such earnestness that I cannot with greater) ; for I am most kindly disposed to him, not only because of all his good qualities, but also because we have common pursuits (use *propter* twice).

18. My own opinion, as I have often told you in my letters, is this—the man who crushes the remnant of this war will bring the whole war to an end (*Lat.*, will be the finisher of, etc.) ; and I hope and believe that you will be that man.

19. I for my part do not cease to exhort *them* to *make* peace ; for even an unjust *peace* is more beneficial than a perfectly just war.

20. I have sent you a copy of Caesar's letter, according to your request (*Lat.*, for you had requested). Many have written to tell me that my *conduct* is completely satisfactory to him. I am content that it should be

so, provided that my conduct is, as it has hitherto been, perfectly honest (*Lat.*, I do nothing basely).

EXERCISE LXXXVIII.

THE RELATIVE—*continued.*   § 222 to 228.

Look out opes ; urgueo ; potissimum : interficio.

1. No one is so old that he does not think he can live a year *longer.*
2. I never yet knew a poet who did not think himself the best *of his kind* (use *nemo* and *videor*).
3. There was not a man who did not protect me in that crisis to the best of his ability.
4. Surely there is no consolation that can assuage my grief.
5. You do not understand in what alarm and what great peril we are *placed.*
6. Who is there who has not an affection for Pompeius ?
7. There was absolutely not a man among the soldiers in the fort who was not wounded (*Lat.*, no one at all).
8. The Stoics say that all are rich who can enjoy the sky and the earth.
9. Why am I to mention things which can be believed by none but eye-witnesses ? (use *credibilis.*)
10. Most people are chiefly inclined to serve one (*Lat.*, him) from whom they expect the greatest *return.*
11. The enemy, beaten in the fight, at once sent envoys to Caesar *to sue* for peace.   They promised to give hostages, and to do what he bade *them.*
12. It is not then by his own *enemies*, for he has none, that he is annoyed.   It is by the enemies of his *friends*, who are numerous and powerful.
13. A slave of P. Clodius was apprehended in the temple of Castor.   Clodius had placed him there to murder Cnaeus Pompeius.

14. Nothing makes *men* so wretched as impiety and crime.
15. Cato says that one who is not a *regular* soldier is not justified in fighting against the enemy (use *ius*).
16. I think there is no man who has heard that fellow's name, who cannot also call to mind his abominable deeds.
17. There is not in this province a single piece of property (*nihil proprium*) left to us by our ancestors in the towns or in the country-districts, which he did not order to be sold.
18. No misfortune befell the state in after days, which they had not seen threatening *her* so long before.
19. Nothing is more difficult than to find a thing which is perfect in its kind in every particular.
20. The plays of Livius do not deserve to be read a second time.

EXAMINATION PAPER S.

On PARTS I. *to* V.

1. Give the Gender and Genitive case of rus, mus, tellus, vulgus, humus, frons, os, mos, vulnus, cor, honor.

2. Give the principal parts of claudo, mordeo, sentio, censeo, queo, aperio, reperio, sino, tundo, iuvo.

3. What is the construction, with Latin Verbs of asking, in the Active and the Passive ? What other Verbs have a similar construction ?

4. What Cases do the following words take :—utor, misereor, credo, potior, expers, dives ?

5. Compare vetus, teres, novus, ater, senex, utilis, maturus, benevolus.

6. What do you understand by the Objective Genitive ? Give instances.

7. What Cases are found with the following Prepositions :—
cis, clam, ob, prae, super ?

8. Render in Latin the following phrases and sentences :—

ENGLISH.	LATIN.
(1) so to say.	that I may so say.
(2) so far as I know.	*as for* what I know (*subj.*).
(3) against the will of Caesar.	
(4) before the consulship of Cicero.	
(5) after the expulsion of the kings.	past participle.
(6) What am I to do ?	
(7) What was I to do ?	
(8) 1 dismissed the messenger at once.	*missum facere.*
(9) to retire.	
(10) as we said before.	impersonal.
(11) Regulus did not rely on his own judgment, but wished the senate to decide.	wished *it* to be the judgment of.
(12) He began to form plans for liberating the state.	
(13) For twenty years I have been waging war against the Romans.	I now wage.
(14) I will say it again and again.	more often.
(15) You decided that one or both of the consuls should proceed to the *seat of* war.	the consuls, one or both.
(16) I will speak as becomes a senator and a Roman.	what is worthy of.
(17) envy of the virtuous.	to envy virtue.
(18) What is such a proof of conceit ?	What is so arrogant ?
(19) the times are such that.	the time is of that kind.
(20) How much did this cost you ?	

EXERCISE LXXXIX.

COMPOUND PRONOUNS. § 229.

Look out transfero ; saeculum ; contingo ; contagio ; conditio ; nego.

1. Some of the soldiers slew themselves near the funeral pile.

2. Did you ever see a more unlucky man ?

3. Ennius translated some passages from Homer.
4. Envy of the virtuous is a kind of blot and blemish of the present age.
5. What? have you ever seen anything like the sun or the moon or the five planets?
6. The house of Isocrates was open to the whole of Greece as a kind of school and manufactory of oratory.
7. The camp of Caesar was close to a forest, and was not more than three hundred paces from the sea.
8. Every animal has its likings and its dislikings (*Lat.*, longs for certain things and flees from certain things).
9. Whatever they say I commend.
10. An accident prevented me from doing that.
11. I promise you all *the aid* that I can *give* to carry out this business.
12. The tribunicial power can inflict much injury *and* much peril on each one among us.
13. Epicurus asserts that no one can live happily who does not live honestly.
14. Let each man think that he is defending in arms not his own person but *our* wives and little children.
15. Did any one ever see Deiotarus dancing or intoxicated?
16. There is no animal, except man, that has any knowledge of God.
17. The Stoics say that nothing is good save that which is right.
18. The taint of that crime has a wider extent than any one supposes.
19. I for my part am in the habit of taking pains that every man should give me instruction about his own profession (*res*).
20. The times are such that every man thinks his own position the most wretched.

CORRELATION OF CLAUSES. § 232.

Look out exsto ; collegium ; summisse ; possessio ; impertio.

1. The best speakers are most in dread of the difficulties of speaking (use *quisque* and *superlative adverbs*).
2. I have made these statements as briefly as they could be made (*passive*).
3. We ought to keep our slaves under command in all places, but especially in *our* provinces.
4. I will accept as much time from you as you will devote to writing.
5. My brother is not so much in fear for his own life as for mine.
6. The consuls have proved to be just as I have often described them to you.
7. What is such a proof of conceit as to attempt to instruct the college of pontiffs on a matter of religion?
8. Your letters have never raised my hopes so much as those of others have.
9. What Aristides was at Athens, such was Fabricius in this city.
10. The higher our rank the more humility let us display in our actions (*Lat.*, let us conduct ourselves).
11. The more they advanced with their work, and the further they put the camp forward, the further was their distance from water.
12. Philosophy has taught us all other lessons (*res*), and especially that which is the hardest *of all to learn*, self-knowledge (*Lat.*, know ourselves).
13. What is so agreeable to *our* intelligence and *our* ears (use supines of *cognosco* and *audio*) as a speech adorned and embellished with wise sentiments and weighty words.

14. The bulk of (*Lat.*, the rest of) the citizens are usually like the chief men in a state.

15. We are disgracefully unprepared in respect of (*a*) men and money too.

16. He lived just as long as he could live happily and peacefully.

17. This affair causes no less annoyance to me than it does to you.

18. The larger an estate is, the more it requires to maintain it.

19. Fortune has supreme influence in all other (*Lat.*, the rest) affairs, but chiefly in war.

20. Show yourself (*impertīre*) to us in the same character as that in which you have hitherto (*iam antea*) presented yourself to the Roman people.

EXAMINATION PAPER T.

On PARTS I. *to* VI.

1. Give the Gender, Dative Singular, and Genitive Plural of species, comes, arbiter, onus, fons, arx, imber.

2. Give the chief Tenses of pareo, increpo, erigo, arceo, capio, occĭdo, pello, repello, cupio, ordior.

3. What are the meanings of the following Prepositions, and with what Cases are they constructed: penes, extra, tenus, pro, citra, propter?

4. Compare frugi, nequam, potis, prosperus, iuvenis, tristis, pulcher, tener.

5. What do you understand by the Subjective Genitive? Give instances.

6. Give instances of some of the uses of the Ablative Case.

7. Explain, with examples, the meaning of the terms *final, temporal,* and *concessive* Conjunctions, and give instances of the moods used with each.

8. Render in Latin the following phrases and sentences:—

English.	Latin.
(1) Many, not to say all.	*ne dicam.*
(2) to say the least.	*levissime.*
(3) to be assured.	to hold for certain.
(4) to devote *one's-self* to literature.	*studere.*
(5) as briefly as I could.	
(6) I have long been desiring.	
(7) in the lifetime of Nero.	
(8) it is of great importance.	
(9) at about the same time.	*fere sub.*
(10) more than 100 years afterwards.	*amplius.*
(11) I pray you, pardon me in this matter.	
(12) You see how the matter stands.	*se habere.*
(13) Pisistratus arranged the books of Homer in their present form.	as we now have *them.*
(14) He insisted on my writing.	*contendere a.*
(15) He was wounded in the service of his country.	received a wound.
(16) I have made up my mind to remain at Rome.	*mihi certum est.*
(17) to do good service to the Roman people.	to deserve well of.
(18) I will reply to your letter briefly.	
(19) I may be deceived.	
(20) I think I shall pay a visit to Caesar.	*ful. inf. pass.*

EXERCISE XCI.—Recapitulatory.

Look out peritus ; percipio ; proprius ; postpono ; comparo ; cogo.

1. Tell me whom you see.
2. I wish I had some advice to give you.
3. Where is the state which has not had bad citizens ?
4. The experienced general perceived what was a hindrance to success.
5. A wise man can distinguish falsehood from truth and the unintelligible from the intelligible.
6. Who is there that avoids things that are expedient ?

7. Do you not remember what I said a little while ago?
8. He declined to state his opinion.
9. Cn. Pompey determined not to allow C. Caesar to be made consul on any other condition but that he would give up his army and the provinces.
10. It is the characteristic of a wise man to do nothing of which he may hereafter repent.
11. The law was so arranged by our forefathers that no Roman citizen can lose his freedom against his will.
12. On my arrival at Rome I at once made a stand against the crime and madness of Antony.
13. Cato used to read even in the senate-house while the senators were assembling.
14. I deemed everything of secondary importance, if I could but obey the injunctions of my father (*Lat.*, I postponed all things, provided that . . .).
15. You will relieve me from great apprehension if there be but a wall between you and me.
16. It is a characteristic of freedom to live as you please. .
17. If I find you here to-morrow, you shall die.
18. If I see you, I hope to get easily over my present difficulties, and those which threaten me *in the future*.
19. Believe me, Brutus, you (*pl.*) will be crushed, if you do not take care.
20. If poverty is an evil, no beggar can be happy.

EXERCISE XCII.

OBLIQUE NARRATION. § 233 to 235.

Turn into the form of Oblique Narration the following sentences, supposing each to be introduced by the words " *He said :* "—

1. I will send you a letter.
2. I shall see you at Athens.

3. I will be your leader.
4. I have finished writing.
5. What have I done?
6. What are you about?
7. Do not fear; I will not forsake thee.
8. Here we shall live a life of safety.
9. If you are wise, you will say nothing.
10. If I dared I would go to Athens.
11. Whither are ye rushing?
12. What is the use of talking?
13. Why are ye come to me?
14. I shall find out to-day how dear I am to the senate.
15. Do ye know any one superior *to me?*
16. My safety is not of so much importance to me as to the country.
17. Will you return to the camp?
18. He said, "I never had a more pleasant draught."
19. I will take good care that the enemy do not attack the city.
20. I gave the empire to my father and to my brother, *and* they have given it back to me.

EXERCISE XCIII.

OBLIQUE NARRATION—*continued.* § 233 to 235.

Look out summa ; vis ; attinet ; affero ; tantumdem.

1. Thereupon this answer was made to the Roman envoys : "The war originated with the Saguntines and not with Hannibal. The Roman people are acting unjustly, if they prefer the people of Saguntum to the time-honoured alliance of the Carthaginians."
2. The story is that in that place Hannibal saw in his sleep (*Lat.*, rest) a youth of celestial mien, who said, "I am sent by Jove to thee to lead thee into Italy : therefore follow *me*, and never at any place turn thine eyes away from me."

3. "We accept the omen," said the consuls, "and pray for such an intention on the part of the enemy, that they should not even defend the rampart."

4. When Hannibal had summoned his soldiers to assemble he encouraged them to fight with the promise of sure rewards (*Lat.*, he proposes sure rewards, for the hope of which they were to fight). "I will give," *said he*, "land in Italy, Africa, Spain, where each man desires, free from taxes for the man who takes it, and for his children. If any one prefers money to land, I will give him an equivalent (*Lat.*, I will satisfy him) in silver. If any of the allies desire to become citizens of Carthage, I will enable them to do so. If any prefer to return home, I will take good care that they shall not wish to change their position with any one of their own countrymen (*Lat.*, that the fortune of any one of their countrymen should be changed with them)."

5. The end of *his* speech was, "The nearer Hannibal is to the hope of bringing the war to a conclusion, so much the more should he be assisted with every resource : for the campaign is *fought* at a distance from home, in the midst of the enemy's land : a vast amount of corn *and* of money is consumed : and so many pitched battles, though they have destroyed the armies of the enemy, have also to some extent impaired the forces of the conqueror. Therefore we must send reinforcements, we must send money to pay and corn *to feed* the soldiers who have done such good service to the Carthaginian nation (*Lat.*, name)."

6. To this Hannibal replied, "So far as the war with the Romans is concerned, as (*si*) the battle of the Trasimenus was more famous than that of the Trebia, as the battle of Cannae was more famous than that of the Trasimenus, so I will overshadow the glories (*Lat.*,

make the remembrance obscure) of Cannae, by a
greater and more splendid victory."

7. Many years before Agrippina had believed and treated
with contempt *a prophecy* of this termination of her
life (*sui*).   For when she consulted the astrologers
about Nero, they replied, " He will get the Empire
(*impero*) and will slay his mother."   Then she rejoined,
" Let him slay *me*, if he do but get the Empire."

8. Envoys from the Germans came to Caesar and spoke as
follows : " We Germans did not take the initiative
(*priores*) in waging war on the Roman people, but
still we do not decline to fight, if we are provoked.
However, what we say is this : We have come against
our will, driven from our homes ; if you Romans
wish to be on good terms with us (*Lat.*, our favour)
we can do you good service (*utiles esse*) as your
friends ; either assign lands to us, or permit us to
retain those which we have won by our arms."

9. Two days after this Ariovistus sends envoys to Caesar
with this message, " I am willing to continue the negoti-
ations (*Lat.*, to 'treat) which we began but did not
finish (*pass.*).   Either (*uti aui*) fix a day for a renewal
of the conference (*Lat.*, for a conference again), or if
you do not like that plan, send one of your lieu-
tenants to me."

10. When Ariovistus saw the envoys sent by Caesar before
him in the camp, he shouted in the hearing (*Lat.*,
presence) of his army, " Why are ye come to me ?   Or
is it as spies ?"   When they attempted to speak, he
stopped them and cast them into chains.

11. The leading men of the Aedui came on an embassy to
Caesar to implore his aid to their state in a time of
sorest need : " Our position," *they said*, " is one of
extreme peril : for whereas the usual practice has
been (*Lat.*, were accustomed to be) for one magistrate

to be elected and to exercise absolute power for a year, two are now holding office, and each asserts that he has been legally elected."

12. Caligula also formed a scheme for destroying the Homeric poems; "For why," said he, "may not I do that which Plato was allowed to do, since he banished the poet (*eum*) from his ideal republic (*Lat.*, the state which he was arranging)?"

13. Caligula was so servile in his behaviour to his grandfather and his grandfather's courtiers (*Lat.*, those near *him*), that it was said, not without reason, "No man was a better slave, or a worse master."

14. Tiberius used to say (*orat. obl.*), "I shall always be as I now am (*Lat.*, like myself), nor shall I ever change my habits as long as I retain my senses."

15. When the commons were hailing Caesar as king he replied, "I am Caesar, and not a king."

16. When Anaxagoras was on his deathbed at Lampsacus, and his friends asked him, "Do you wish, in case anything happens to you, to be carried into your native land to Clazomenae?" "There is no need *for that*," said he, "since the distance to Hades is exactly the same from every place (*undique*)."

17. When Dionysius had landed on the Peloponnesus, and paid a visit to the shrine of the Olympian Jove, he took away from the god (*is*) a golden mantle of great weight, remarking, "A golden mantle is oppressive in summer, *and* cold in winter," and he threw over him a woollen cloak,—"for that," said he, "is *suitable* to every season."

18. Socrates, the wisest *of men*, used to say, "I know nothing, except this very fact that I know nothing; other people are ignorant of this also."

19. When Antisthenes was asked, "What gain have you derived from philosophy?" he replied, "To be able to talk to myself."

20. Agesilaus, intending to go across Thrace, sent messengers to the king of Macedonia, to ask this question, " Am I to go through the land of foes or friends ?" When the king replied, " I will consider," he rejoined, " Let him consider (*Lat.*, Let the consultation then be made) ; we in the meanwhile will continue our march."

EXERCISE XCIV.

DISJUNCTIVE QUESTIONS—Ne quidem, etc. § 237.

1. Do you regard me as a waiting-maid or as a daughter ?
2. Does your memory fail you in this matter (*Lat.*, have you but little memory of this), or did I not understand *you* fully ?
3. Are we talking of a commander of the Roman people or of Hannibal ?
4. Did I try to escape death at that time ? Or was there any event which I thought more to be desired by me ?
5. Is it money that makes you more haughty, or the fact that the commander asks your advice ?
6. If you are unwell (*fut.*), it makes no difference whether I be well or ill.
7. Is it to my advantage to return, or is it better for me to stop on *here ?*
8. A disgraceful life does not admit even an honourable death (*Lat.*, leaves no room for).
9. Even to the Romans, the victory was not without sorrow (*Lat.*, joyful).
10. Even at Rome the name of Caractacus was not unknown to fame.
11. Did he force you to buy, who did not even encourage you to do so ?

12. Even in that critical moment not (*Lat.*, not even at that time) a man gave way, but all were surrounded and slain.

13. It makes no difference whether I go (*venīre*) there now or ten years hence.

14. I will write to you at greater length, when I find more leisure.

15. There is no evil, no crime, which that woman did not wish, desire, plan, and bring about against her son (*dat.*).

16. Carneades never maintained an argument (*res*) which he did not prove, *and* never opposed one which he did not upset.

17. I have always made it my first care (*Lat.*, laboured) to be worthy of an honour, my second to be thought *worthy ;* that, which with most men stands (*est*) first, has *ever* been in the third place with me (*Lat.*, third for me),— the honour itself.

18. It is also useful to make frequent practice of extempore speaking : but it (*illud*) is more useful, by taking time for meditation, to speak with more preparation and precision.

19. Pray tell me whether he was unwilling or unable to approach the city ?

20. I never thought there was any matter in which it made the slightest (*tantulum*) difference, whether you did it by agents or with your own hands (*Lat.*, by yourself).

XCV.—GENERAL SENTENCES.

1. It was on that very narrow strait which parts Europe from Asia, at the furthest extremity of Europe, that the Greeks built Byzantium. When they consulted the Pythian Apollo as to where they should found a city, the oracle replied[1] that they were to seek a home

---

[1] an oracle was returned.

opposite the land of the blind. This dark saying pointed to the people of Chalcedon,[1] inasmuch as they, though they arrived[2] there first, and saw before others the advantages of the position,[3] chose the worse.

2. When Solon was asked why he had not appointed a punishment for parricide,[4] he replied, " I did not suppose that any one would commit the crime."

3. I do not want you to tell me why Sextus Roscius killed his father : I want you to tell me how he killed him.

4. It is said that Thales of Miletus, desiring to put those who blamed him in the wrong,[5] and to prove that even a philosopher, if it suited his purpose,[6] could turn an honest penny,[7] bought up all the olive-plantations[8] in the district of Miletus before they came into flower.[9]   Probably he was led by some observation[10] to know that there would be an abundant crop[11] of olives.   He too is said to have been the first to foretell an eclipse of the sun, which happened in the reign of Astyages.

5. Physicians, pilots, and farmers too, foresee many future events, and yet I do not give the name of divination to any one of their prognostications,[12] nor even to that by which Anaximander the natural philosopher warned[13] the Spartans to leave their city and their dwellings, and to keep watch in arms in the open fields, because an earthquake was at hand, that being the time when the whole city was turned into a heap of ruins.[14]

6. When Aristotle was asked what profit men get by lying,[15]

---

[1] the Chalcedonians were pointed to by that dark saying.
[2] advecti.
[3] abl. abs.
[4] one who killed a parent.
[5] to convict his censurers.
[6] if it were an advantage to him.
[7] make money.
[8] singular.   [9] began to flower.
[10] observed by some knowledge.
[11] fertility.
[12] I call no one of these divination.
[13] passive.   [14] fell in a heap.
[15] liars make.

he replied, "That men who speak the truth are not believed."

7. Nasica went to pay a visit to Ennius the poet. When he asked at[1] the door for Ennius, a waiting-maid answered, "He is not at home." Nasica perceived that the girl said this by her master's order, and that he was in the house. A few days after Ennius paid a visit to Nasica, and asked for him at the gate. Nasica cries out, "He is not at home." Then Ennius said, "How? do I not know your voice?" Nasica replied, "You are an impudent fellow. When I asked for you, I believed your maid *when she told me* that you were not at home; do you not believe me *when I tell you* myself?"

8. Cato was hit by a slave carrying a chest, and the man cried out, "Have a care!" whereupon Cato asked him whether he was carrying anything besides the chest.

9. Spurius Carvilius limped terribly from a wound received in the service of the state, and for that reason was ashamed to appear in public. His mother said to him,[2] "Why do you not go out, dear Spurius, so that at every step you take, the remembrance of your glorious deeds may come into your thoughts?"[3]

10. A common[4] soldier in the Theban army having caught sight of the Spartans approaching through a narrow pass in the hills, said to Pelopidas, "We have fallen among the enemy." "Rather say," he replied, "they have fallen among us."

11. When Themistocles was asked whether he had rather be Achilles or Homer, he replied, "Tell me first whether you would rather be a victor in the Olympic games or the herald who proclaims the victors."

---

[1] from.   [2] to Spurius Carvilius . . . his mother said.
[3] *it* may come into *your* mind *about* your glorious deeds (*genitive*).
[4] quispiam.

12. On the arrival of Cicero in the camp of Pompey, they said to him, "You have come late." "Not at all late," he replied, "for I see nothing ready here as yet."

13. It was the habit of Augustus rarely to refuse an invitation[1] to a banquet. On one occasion[2] he was entertained with a very scanty and quite commonplace[3] dinner. On taking leave of his host,[4] he just whispered in his ear, "I did not think we were such intimate friends."

14. Quintus Scaevola asked that the selling price of a farm, which he wanted to buy,[5] might be named[6] to him. When the vendor complied with his request, he said, "I think it is worth more," and he increased the price by[7] a hundred thousand *sesterces*.

15. Livius Salinator, after losing Tarentum, still kept the citadel, and fought many brilliant[8] fights. A few years after Fabius Maximus retook that town. Salinator begged him to remember that he had retaken Tarentum by his assistance. "How can I help remembering that?" said Maximus; "I never should have retaken it, unless you had lost it."

16. Spurinna the soothsayer warned Caius Caesar to be on his guard against a great peril which would not extend[9] beyond the Ides of March. As Caesar was on his way to the senate on that day, he chanced to meet Spurinna, and addressed him thus: "How say you now? Have not the Ides of March come?" "They have come," he replied, "but they have not gone."

17. As Spartacus was setting out with all his troops to meet Crassus,[10] a man offered him a horse as a gift. But

---

[1] one inviting.   [2] by a certain man.   [3] almost daily.
[4] when he was dismissed by his entertainer.   [5] was a buyer.
[6] to name the selling price = semel indicare.   [7] added to the price.
[8] adverb.   [9] be prolonged.   [10] moving all his forces to Crassus.

he said, " If I win the day, I shall have horses in abundance from the enemy ; and, if I am beaten, this horse [1] will be of no service to me." So saying he plunged his sword into the horse and killed it.[2]

18. As the court [3] was considering what punishment [4] Socrates deserved, " I," said he, " am of opinion that for my acts I deserve to be maintained at the public expense [5] in the Prytaneum." This was an honour usually paid to those who had done eminent service to the state.

19. Augustus died in the very same chamber in which his father Octavius died, in the consulship of Sextus Pompeius and Sextus Appuleius, on the 19th of August, at 3 P.M. He was seventy-six years of age, within thirty-five days.

20. Charillus was asked how it was that Lycurgus had made so few laws for the Spartans. " Because," he replied, " men who talk but little require but few laws."

21. When Xenophon asked Socrates to advise him whether he should follow Cyrus, " My advice," he replied, " is but that of a man : on matters of doubt and uncertainty I hold that we should refer to Apollo."

22. The enemy, being vanquished in the fight, had no sooner returned from their flight than they sent envoys without delay to Caesar to treat for peace. They promised to give hostages, and to carry out all his commands.

23. Cato believed that one who could talk like honest men,[6] could also act like them.

24. A painter who had a commission to paint a horse rolling,[7] painted the horse running. When the man who gave him the commission complained of this, the

---

[1] nec hic.   [2] slew the horse, pierced through with his sword.   [3] judges.
[4] disceptare inter se.   [5] publicitus.   [6] imitate the speech.
[7] had received a horse to be painted with the appearance of one rolling.

painter said, with a smile, " Turn the picture upside down." When this was done the horse seemed to be rolling and not running.

25. Socrates was told that a certain person gave him a bad character.[1] " Doubtless," said he to his informer, " the man has not learnt to speak properly."

26. Caecilius Metellus was planning an attack with his army on a strong position.[2] A centurion said to him, " If you are willing to sacrifice the lives of but ten men, you will take the place." Thereupon Metellus asked him whether he was willing to be one of the ten.

27. Cato used to say, " Fools are more useful to wise men[3] than wise men to fools : for wise men, by[4] easily perceiving the mistakes of fools, and avoiding them, become more wary ; whereas it is not so with fools,[5] inasmuch as they do not see that they can imitate the sage conduct of the wise."

28. King Archelaus invited Socrates to his court, and offered him many inducements. The answer of Socrates was : " I do not like to visit a man from whom I am to receive favours, without being able to make him a return."[6]

29. Cato used to compare the Roman people to a flock of sheep, which obey[7] no particular *sheep*, but follow the leader of the whole flock. " Thus you," said he, " allow yourselves, when assembled here, to be driven and led by these men, from whom not one of you would ask advice in private life."[8] (Relative clause first.)

30. Cato, observing that many persons had statues erected in

---

[1] speak ill of.
[2] to move his army on a fortified place.
[3] confer more advantage on.
[4] dum.
[5] at stultos non item.
[6] to give back equal *favours* to him.
[7] obtempero.
[8] summon to counsel privately.

their honour,[1] remarked, "I would rather men should ask in my case why no statue has been put up in honour of Cato, than *that they should ask* why one has been put up to him."

31. When the fortifications of the camp were finished, C. Sulpicius Gallus, a tribune of the second legion, who had been praetor the year before, obtained the consul's permission to collect the soldiers in assembly, and made this announcement to them :[2] "To-night— and let no one[3] regard it as a prodigy—the moon will be eclipsed from the second hour to the fourth. As this happens in the course of nature at fixed times, it can be known beforehand and predicted." On the night preceding the 4th of September the moon was eclipsed at the hour named, and the Roman soldiers thought[4] the wisdom of Gallus almost divine. Upon the Macedonians, on the other hand, it had the effect of[5] a dismal portent, foreboding the fall of their kingdom and the ruin of their nation ; nor did their prophets *explain it* otherwise.

32. Envoys from many states of Greece and Asia arrived at Rome at the same time. The first that had audience[6] were the Athenians. They represented that they had sent what ships and soldiers they had to the consul Publius Licinius, and the praetor Caius Lucretius, who did not think proper to employ these forces, but ordered[7] them to furnish one hundred thousand *measures* of corn. Notwithstanding the sterility of their soil,[8] and that they fed even the farm-labourers with imported grain, yet, that they might not fail in their duty, they had made up that quantity, and were

---

[1] statues of many were erected.   [2] pronuntiare.   [3] ne quis.
[4] Historic Infinitive.   [5] moveo ut.   [6] were introduced.
[7] which they not having used ordered.
[8] though they were ploughing a barren land.

ready to perform [1] any other services that might be required of them.

33. The year was remarkable for drought and dearth. It is on record that not a drop of rain fell [2] for six months. In that year also, while the labourers on the farm of Lucius Petillius the notary, at the foot of Janiculum, were turning up the soil somewhat deeper than usual, two stone chests were found, each about eight feet long and four wide, having lids soldered down [3] with lead. Each chest had an inscription in Latin and in Greek, *to the effect* that in one Numa Pompilius, king of Rome, was buried, and that the books of Numa Pompilius was deposited in the other.

34. A few days after this the Celtiberians pitched their camp about two miles from that place, at the foot of a hill. When the Roman commander observed their approach, he sent his brother Marcus Fulvius with two squadrons of the cavalry of the allies towards the camp of the enemy to reconnoitre. He was ordered to approach as close as he could to the intrenchment, that he might observe the size *of the camp*, to avoid a battle, and to retire in case he saw the cavalry of the enemy sallying forth. He carried out these orders. [4]

35. Licinius Mucianus held Syria with [5] four legions. He was a man equally notorious in prosperity and in adversity. In his youth he had eagerly courted the friendship of the great ; afterwards, when his fortunes were broken, and his position unsafe, when he also suspected that Claudius was angry with him, he was sent away [6] to a remote part of Asia, and he was as little removed from being an exile as he was afterwards from being an emperor. His character was a mixture [7] of self-

---

[1] praestare. [2] It has been handed to memory that it never rained.
[3] bound fast. [4] he did as it had been directed.
[5] and. [6] put aside. [7] mixtus.

indulgence, application, courtesy, and pride, of bad and good qualities : too much addicted to pleasure in his leisure hours,[1] under press of business[2] his virtues were great. His public conduct was praiseworthy :[3] his private life[4] had a bad repute. But with those under his rule, with those about his person,[5] and with his colleagues, he had great influence[6] by his many winning ways,[7] and he was one for whom it would have been more easy[8] to hand the empire to another than to get it[9] *for himself.*

36. When Antiochus the Great, king of Asia, after being vanquished by Scipio, had been ordered to confine his dominions within the limits of Mount Taurus,[10] and had lost the whole of our present province of Asia,[11] he was wont to say (*orat. obl.*), "The Roman people have dealt kindly with me, in that I have been relieved of too great a charge, and am left with[12] a kingdom of moderate dimensions."[13]

37. But as Regulus deserves praise for keeping his oath, so those ten men, sent by Hannibal to the senate after the battle of Cannae (they having taken an oath that, if they should fail to obtain[14] the ransom of the prisoners, they would return to the camp which the Carthaginians had won), are blameworthy, supposing that they did not return.

38. Hannibal had in his hands 8000 men. He had not taken them prisoners in the battle, nor had they escaped from the peril of death ; but they had been left in the camp by the consuls Paulus and Varro.

---

[1] excessive pleasures when he was at leisure.
[2] as often as he had business.   [3] you would commend *him* publicly.
[4] secreta.   [5] nearest.   [6] powerful.
[7] various allurements.   [8] expeditius.   [9] obtain.
[10] to reign up to Taurus.   [11] this Asia which is now our province.
[12] utor.   [13] moderate limits of a kingdom.
[14] unless they succeeded with regard to.

The senate did not think it right that these men should be ransomed, though it would have cost but a small sum. The reason was that our soldiers should feel[1] that they must conquer or die.

39. It is a well-known fact that Olympias gave birth to Alexander on the night in which the temple of Diana of Ephesus was burnt to the ground, and that when day was breaking the Magi cried out, "Last night the plague and destroyer[2] of Asia was born."

40. Dionysius, after plundering the shrine of Proserpine at Locri, was sailing to Syracuse. As he sped along[3] on his course with a fair wind, "Do you see, my friends," said he, "how favourable a voyage is granted by the immortal gods to the robbers of temples?"

41. Yet indeed so crabbed and hard to please are we, that Demosthenes himself is not good enough[4] for us; for though he is pre-eminent above all in every kind of oratory, yet he does not always satisfy my ear.[5]

42. Publius Scipio, who first gained the name of Africanus, was wont to say, as we learn from the writings of Cato,[6] who lived about the same time (*orat. obl.*), "I am never less at leisure[7] than when I am at leisure, and never less alone than when I am alone."

43. Themistocles was consulted *by a friend* whether he should give his daughter in marriage to a worthy man who had but little money, or to a wealthy man who had but an indifferent character. "I," said he, "would rather have a man without money than money without a man."

44. In that engagement seventy-four of our cavalry fell,[8]

---

[1] it might be implanted in.   [2] destruction.   [3] tenere.
[4] satisfies.   [5] fill my ears.
[6] Cato who . . . has written that Pub. Scipio. . . .   [7] otiosus.
[8] interficiuntur.

and among them the brave Aquitanian, Piso.   He
was a man of very good family, for his grandfather
had exercised kingly power[1] in his own state, and
received from our senate the style of Friend.   Going
to the aid of his brother, who had been hemmed in
by the enemy, he rescued him from danger.   His
horse was wounded and he was thrown to the ground.
He made a stout resistance as long as he could, but
at length he was surrounded, and fell after receiving
many wounds.   His brother, who had by this time
got out of the fray, perceiving this from a distance,
set spurs to his horse,[2] charged the enemy, and was
slain.

45. The Gauls as a nation[3] are exceedingly scrupulous[4] in
religious matters.   Hence it is that they who suffer
from dangerous diseases, and they who are engaged
in fighting and perilous occupations, either offer
human sacrifices or vow that they will offer them, and
they employ the Druids to assist[5] in such sacrifices.
For they think that atonement can be made[6] in no
other way to the immortal gods, save by giving a
human life for a human life.   They have also sacrifices
of the same kind appointed for the benefit of the
community.[7]

46. The Druids administer the law in[8] almost all disputes,
public and private.   If any crime has been committed,
if murder has been done, if there is any dispute about
succession to property or the boundaries of land,
they[9] decide the case.   If any man, in private life or
public office, does not abide by their decision, they
cut him off from the sacrifices.   This is with them

---

[1] had obtained the kingdom.
[2] incitato equo.
[3] the whole nation of the Gauls.
[4] devoted.
[5] as assistants.   [6] be appeased.
[7] publicly.
[8] arrange concerning.
[9] iidem.

the most severe punishment. Men who are under this ban are deemed ungodly and wicked; all people shun their company, *none* will associate or converse with them[1] for fear of infection.[2] If they ask for justice it is not given,[3] and they are not allowed a share in any public office.[4]

47. Judges are also bribed by gifts; and for that reason, in the statutes passed in reference to extortion, punishment was assigned to those who received money in respect of a judicial sentence.[5] Plutarch tells us that at Thebes in the olden time statues of the judges were set up in a public place, and that these statues had no hands, to indicate that the judges ought to receive nothing from any one. Moreover, the statue of the President of the Court had no eyes, because they thought that in some cases judges were diverted from a right judgment by personal appearances.[6]

48. I was surprised by so long a letter in your own handwriting, for I am well aware how inconvenient it is for you to write. Consequently, in the midst of the extreme delight that I had from the letter, the thought of your eyesight[7] caused me some pain. Yet surely even this shows me clearly[8] the warmth of your affection for me, since, knowing, as you do, what intense enjoyment[9] I derive from your letters, to gratify[10] me in that way you do not spare even the eyes, which nature designed to be our dearest *possessions.*

49. It is a fine remark of Aristotle, that when a man is called a miser by some people, and a spendthrift by

---

1 shrink from their approach and speech.
2 lest they receive some harm from contagion.　　3 redditur.
4 nor is any honour communicated *to them.*　　5 for judging a case.
6 by the very sight of persons.　　7 that which I thought about your eyes.
8 by this is seen clearly.　　9 suavitas.　　10 explere.

others, the natural inference is[1] is that he is a generous fellow.

50. It is one thing to write biographies and another to write
a history. The biographer describes carefully and
minutely a man's domestic life, his behaviour to his
wife, his children, his intimate friends, his guests, his
mode of living and his style of dress.[2] The historian
either omits all these matters, or touches on them
lightly and cautiously, as accessories to his main
business ;[3] in pursuance of his chief object[4] he dis-
cusses matters of public interest only. This we may
learn from Plutarch himself, who, even while writing
the lives of eminent men, tells us that he is not
writing history.

51. At the same time the centurion L. Fabius and the men
who had scaled the wall with him were surrounded,
slain, and cast headlong from the wall. M. Petreius,
a centurion of the same legion, tried to cut his way
through the gates. Overpowered by numbers, and
despairing of his own life,[5] for he had already received
many wounds,[6] he cried to the men of his company[7]
who had followed him, " Since I cannot save you and
myself at the same time, I am determined to take
thought for your safety,[8] seeing that in my eagerness
to win renown[9] I have led you into danger. When
the chance presents itself, take thought for yourselves." Saying this he dashed into the midst of the
enemy, struck down two of them, and pushed the
others a little way from the gate. His men tried to
relieve him, but he cried, " It is in vain that you
attempt to save my life, for my blood and strength

---

[1] it serves as an argument.   [2] what food and dress of the body he used.
[3] as an accession, as though doing another thing.   [4] of set purpose.
[5] despairing for himself.   [6] abl. abs.   [7] manipulares.
[8] at least I will surely take thought for your life.
[9] led on by desire for fame.

are failing; therefore get away while you have the chance, and return to the legion." So fighting on after a while he fell and saved his men.

52. When Caesar was informed of their plans he led his army to the river Thames within the territory of Cassivellaunus. This river can be crossed on foot in one place only, and there with difficulty. On his arrival at the spot he perceived that a large force of the enemy was drawn up on the opposite bank, that the bank had been strengthened by sharp stakes pointed towards the stream,[1] and that stakes of the same construction[2] beneath the water were hidden by the current. Caesar learnt these arrangements from the prisoners and deserters, and sending forward his cavalry in haste he ordered the legions to follow close after them. But the soldiers pressed on with such speed and spirit, though they had nothing but their heads above water, that the enemy, unable to sustain the attack of the legions and the cavalry, forsook the bank and fled.[3]

53. When they heard the shouts in the rear, the Germans, seeing their countrymen cut down, threw away their arms, forsook their colours, and rushed out of the camp. When they reached the junction of the Moselle and the Rhine, further flight being hopeless, and many of them having been slain, the rest plunged headlong into the stream and perished there, overpowered by fear, by exhaustion, and by the force of the current. Our own troops, without the loss of a single man—very few were wounded—returned to their camp.

54. For a long time the phalanx was cut down in front, on the flanks, and in the rear. At last the men who had escaped from the hands of the enemy, fleeing without

---

[1] praefixis. [2] kind. [3] committed themselves to flight.

their arms to the sea, some even entering the water,
stretched out their hands to those on board[1] the fleet,
and humbly begged their lives.   Then perceiving
boats hastening towards them[2] on all sides from the
ships, and supposing they were coming to pick them
up, rather to capture than to kill them, they advanced
further, some of them even swimming, into the
water.   But when the men in the boats cut them
down as enemies,[3] all who were able swam back again
to land,[4] and fell into a different and more terrible
form of destruction,[5] for the elephants, urged by their
drivers to the beach, trod them down and crushed
them as they came ashore (*Lat.*, coming out).

55. When I hear those people complain of the obscurity of
Tacitus, I consider how ready men are to shift their
own faults on other persons, and how easily they
fasten blame on anything but themselves.[6] I remember, too, *the story*, so pleasantly told by Seneca,[7] of an
old gentleman who, when his eyesight was failing by
natural decay,[8] on coming into a room was wont to
say, "This room is badly lighted : the windows
should have been made larger." I have a friend of
my own—long may I have him !—one of the most
learned men of the day, so old, that at this time, to
use Juvenal's phrase, he is almost counting his years
with his right hand. When he had become somewhat deaf through age, he often complained to me in
sober earnestness of a bad habit that was coming into
vogue, for people to talk in a lower voice now-a-days
than they used.

---

[1] in.   [2] concurrere.
[3] they were cut down in hostile fashion from the boats.
[4] seeking the land again by swimming back.   [5] more foul plague.
[6] how much more easily they blame all other things *rather* than themselves.
[7] about whom (*masc.*) Seneca narrates wittily.
[8] used his eyes less conveniently through the fault of age.

56. Now if any one supposes that under the very worst[1] emperors men of eminent virtue did not flourish, he is greatly mistaken. Germanicus, not to mention the rest, lived in the reign of Tiberius, and I hold that no one even of the famous Romans of old was superior[2] to Germanicus in every kind of excellence. Seneca lived under Claudius, and though perhaps no one was equal to Seneca, yet many were like him. The age of Nero had many whose virtue his vices could scarcely rival.

57. As on the top of Aetna, where the fire burns most fiercely, men tell us that the grass in its vicinity is also most luxuriant, as though nature had a struggle with herself, and was unwilling that the productiveness of the soil should be mastered by the heat of the neighbouring flames, so where the greatest vices are dominant, the greatest virtues generally break forth to fight against them,[3] and, though they may be unable to get the mastery, yet not to allow their foes to triumph[4] without a struggle.

58. When Caractacus stood before the tribunal he spoke as follows :—" Had my moderation in[5] prosperity been equal to my rank and fortune, I should have visited this city rather as a friend than as a captive : nor wouldst thou have disdained to receive under a treaty of peace a man of high lineage, the ruler of many nations. My present condition is as glorious to thee as it is degrading to me. I had horses, men, arms, wealth : is it to be wondered at that I was unwilling to part with them ?[6] Though you *Romans* desire universal empire,[7] it does not follow that all men will accept slavery. Had I been handed over[8] at once as

---

[1] most corrupt.
[2] I hold superior = I prefer.
[3] to take up a contest with them.
[4] grant a triumph to their foes.
[5] genitive.
[6] lost them unwillingly.
[7] to rule all men.
[8] imperfect past.

a prisoner, neither my fortune nor your fame would have been conspicuous, and oblivion would follow my punishment : whereas if you keep me unhurt, I shall be an everlasting monument of clemency." Thereupon Caesar granted pardon to him, his wife, and his brothers.

59. Porsena, being repulsed in his first attempt, changed his plan of assaulting the city into a blockade,[1] and having placed a garrison in Janiculum, he pitched his own camp in the plain on the banks of the Tiber. He collected ships from all quarters,[2] to serve as[3] a guard, that he might stop the conveyance of corn[4] to Rome, and also that he might, as opportunities arose, carry his soldiers over the river in different places to forage.

60. By far the most important and most toilsome of all the works was a mine that they began to drive[5] into the enemy's citadel. To provide against the interruption of this work, and also to guard against[6] the exhaustion of the same men by constant subterraneous toil, Camillus divided the pioneers into six parties : six hours were assigned to each in succession for the work : and they never ceased working[7] by night and by day till they made a way into the citadel.

61. The poets never introduce the augur Tiresias, whom they represent as a wise man, bewailing his blindness ; but, on the other hand,[8] Homer, having conceived Polyphemus as savage and brutal, goes so far as to represent[9] him conversing with a ram, and praising (*infin.*) the good fortune of the animal, who could walk whithersoever he would, and could touch what-

---

[1] abl. abs.   [2] abl. abs.   [3] both as . . . and.
[4] not to allow any corn to be conveyed.   [5] began to be driven.
[6] neu.   [7] it was never dropped.
[8] ut vero.   [9] even represents.

ever he pleased.   The poet is right : [1] for the Cyclops himself is not a whit more sensible than the ram.

62. Departing from Italy, I sailed with the fleet [2] from Brundisium at sunrise : at the ninth hour I reached [3] Corcyra with my whole squadron.   On the fifth day after I offered sacrifice to Apollo at Delphi, in behalf of myself, of *your* armies and fleets.   On the fifth day after leaving Delphi I arrived in the camp, and there, having taken the command of the army,[4] and made changes in certain arrangements, which greatly hindered success, I advanced, because the enemy's position was impregnable, and it was impossible to force the king to give battle.   *Marching* between his garrisons, I made my way through the pass to Petra, and having compelled the king to fight, I defeated him in a pitched battle.   I brought Macedonia under the Roman power, and in fifteen days I finished a war, which [5] four of my predecessors in the consulship had conducted during a space of four years in such a way that each one handed it on to his successor [6] more formidable than he found it.

63. When the enemy perceived that they were disappointed in their hope of storming the town and crossing the river, when they [7] also saw that our men did not advance to less favourable ground to give battle, and when *they found that* their supply of corn began to fail, they called a council, and determined that their best course was to return [8] each to his own home.

64. I send you a few verses.   They are not very good, but just what you might expect from a man who never had a turn for poetry,[9] who is now old, and who is

---

[1] he indeed rightly.
[2] solvere classem.
[3] tenere.
[4] accepto exercitu.
[5] relative clause first.
[6] they always delivered to the successor.
[7] neque.
[8] reverti.
[9] ever a poet.

constantly occupied with business of his own and of his friends.

65. I am longing for leisure, and when once I am able to attain it, nothing shall induce me to part with it.[1] Not that I intend to give myself up to idleness, but when I have obtained relief from other cares, I intend to put a final polish,[2] to the best of my ability, on many works, begun long ago, that are lying in my desk.[3] But what am I about? why do I make so long a forecast? Perhaps death will break in on my designs.[4] Still, come when it may, I would rather have it find me busy than idle.

66. The Corinthians sent an embassy to offer the freedom[5] of their city to Alexander the Great. Alexander laughed at such a compliment,[6] whereupon one of the envoys remarked, "You and Hercules are the only persons on whom we have conferred the freedom of our city." When the king heard this, he willingly accepted the proffered honour.

67. When King Porus, after his defeat by Alexander, was asked by that *monarch* at the conclusion of the fight, "How shall I treat you?" he replied, "Like a king." Upon the further inquiry from Alexander,[7] "Have *you* any other *request to make?*" Porus replied, "The words 'like a king' include everything."

68. Alexander had among the prisoners of war an Indian, so famous[8] for his skill in archery, that it was even said he could shoot an arrow through a ring. The king bade him give a proof of his skill, and on his refusal ordered him to be put to death. As the man was being led *to execution*, he told his escort[9] that he

---

[1] nothing shall be so important that I should allow myself to be torn away from it.　　　[2] to complete and thoroughly polish.　　　[3] by me.
[4] on me meditating these plans.　　　[5] by envoys . . . offered the freedom.
[6] kind of service.　　　[7] Alexander making the further suggestion.
[8] cum primis celeber.　　　[9] by whom he was being led.

had had no practice for many days, and therefore feared that he might miss his mark. When this was reported to Alexander, and it appeared [1] that the man had refused not from insolence but through fear of disgrace, *the king*, struck with admiration of his passion for renown,[2] released him and gave him a reward, because he deemed it better to face death than to be thought undeserving of his reputation.

69. When Aristippus was asked what profit he had derived from the study of philosophy, he replied, " The power that I have of talking freely with whom I will."

70. Aristippus, when a man asked him what advantage a good education would confer on his son, replied, " This, if nothing more, that he will not sit in the theatre as a stone upon a stone." On another occasion when a man,[3] who thought the fee demanded for his son's tuition too large, said, " With the sum you ask I can buy myself a slave :" " No doubt you can," said Aristippus, bantering him, " if not more ;[4] in buying one *slave* you will have two."

71. By justice, states, commencing from small and humble beginnings, have in a short time attained to great power : by injustice the most flourishing and wealthy *communities* have in yet shorter time been utterly ruined.[5] For it is not by those adamantine chains, of which the elder Dionysius was always talking,[6] force and fear, that great empires are kept, but by justice and equity. And therefore wisely did the Persians deal with the eldest of the king's children, who was brought up as the heir-apparent,[7] in assigning[8] to him divers [9] instructors in morality, and one in particular to teach him justice.

---

[1] quod. [2] his disposition eager for renown. [3] idemque alteri.
[4] amplius. [5] concidere. [6] had frequently on his lips.
[7] to the hope of the kingdom. [8] deal in assigning = used to give. [9] alii.

72. When Leon, the son of Eurycratides, was asked in what city one could possibly (*tandem*) live with safety, "In that," he replied, "whose inhabitants have neither too much nor too little ; where justice flourishes, *and* injustice is weak."

73. The friends of Titus warned him that he was promising more to his petitioners than he could perform. His answer was "No man ought to depart with a sad heart[1] from an interview with Caesar."

74. When Xerxes saw the Hellespont quite covered with his ships, and all the shore crowded with men, he boasted of his happiness,[2] and anon burst into tears. Artabanus, the king's uncle, who had advised him not to make the expedition, was surprised at the sudden change, and ventured to ask the cause. Xerxes replied, "The thought struck me,[3] how short human life is, seeing that of all this vast host not one will be alive a hundred years hence."

75. After the expulsion of Dionysius the younger from his kingdom one asked him what good Plato and philosophy had done[4] to him. (*Direct*) "To bear," he replied, "with equanimity[5] this great reverse of fortune." Nor did he lay violent hands on himself, as others often do, but he opened a grammar school at Corinth.

76. I deem it almost superfluous in this place to beg you to favour me with your attention?[6] Surely you have come for that purpose : and just as a bath-keeper would act absurdly[7] in begging people with earnest entreaties[8] to take a bath when he sees they have come into his bath-house for that purpose,[9] so I think

---

[1] sad.
[2] boasted that he was happy.
[3] Subiit.
[4] Quid profuit.
[5] easily.
[6] hear me attentively.
[7] be ridiculous.
[8] many prayers.
[9] for the sake of washing.

it would be absurd for me[1] to ask you to do that which you have met here to do. Such is the custom of public speakers, who, even when they are quite sure they will be listened to with earnest attention, ask for a favourable hearing :[2] not because they think it necessary to do so, but because they think that by not doing so they have broken the rules[3] of their art. It is my duty to try to bring under your notice things worth hearing : it is yours not to allow them to flit away, but weighing each carefully, to let them sink deep[4] into your minds. I have taken pains to come not unprepared to perform my part of the business :[5] I am sure that you too, with your usual kindness and attention, are prepared to listen to me fully *and* freely (*Lat.*, of your own free will).

77. Even if no rewards had been held out for literature, still learning deserves to be loved for her own sake : and nothing is more disgraceful in a gentleman than ignorance of subjects, the knowledge of which cannot be acquired without the study of books.[6] The pleasure that is derived from sin soon passes away, but it leaves a lasting sorrow in the soul : whereas the pains that are bestowed on good actions,[7] though soon past and gone,[8] leave in the soul a reminiscence of themselves full of the noblest and truest enjoyment.

78. I wish you would take pains to let me know[9] what author you are now enjoying, whether it be Cicero, or Terence, or (as I would rather *hear*) both. You should also be careful to use in your letters to me the idiomatic phrases[10] that you have observed in your writings.

---

[1] Ego mihi videor ridiculus fore.
[2] attention.
[3] have acted against the precepts.
[4] penitus demittere.
[5] quod est mearum partium.
[6] sine litteris.
[7] in rebus honestis collocatus.
[8] itself indeed passes away (effugio).
[9] diligenter scribere.
[10] kinds of speaking.

By this means I shall be assured[1] that you have read them carefully.

79. Observe a proof of my affection for you in the fact, that though I have heard from many correspondents to-day, I have thought it my first and chief duty to reply to your letter. Do not suppose, my dear Alexander, that your own father loves you more than I do. If you ask me why I have this strong affection for you, I protest[2] that I can give you no other reason, except my belief that I have noticed in you talents of a high order, and capable, if you be so minded, of the highest achievements.[3]

80. Your son left me yesterday morning, and his tutor went with him. I entertained both[4] to the best of my ability with kindness and attention. It seemed to me that *the lad* had quite got rid of the roughness which at one time threatened, in my opinion, to grow upon him.[5] I *must* also *tell you* that I examined him, though not very minutely, as to his progress in his studies.[6] Shall I speak without reserve?[7] I thought he knew more than his tutor.

81. As among grown-up people they lead the easiest life who are most in fear of the laws, and on the other hand they who have no fear of the laws are[8] in constant dread of accusers and judges: so among boys they who are most in dread of the commands of their masters are least in dread of a flogging.

82. Pollux shared his immortality with his brother Castor, so that they died and came to life again alternately.

83. Otho reigned ninety days. Though he had lived a most

---

[1] So that this very practice (*res*) may give me an assurance of your diligence in reading them.   [2] ne vivam.

[3] natum ad omnia summa.   [4] both were cared for.

[5] I was slightly-fearful lest it should increase with age.

[6] I tried what progress (*pl.*) he had made in letters.

[7] Would you have me talk openly with you?   [8] versor.

abandoned life,[1] he died with great honour, and he laid down most nobly the government which he had most foully[2] usurped.

84. It is far better and far more in accordance with justice that one should die for many, than many for one. I for my part had rather be a Mutius or a Curtius than a Marius or a Sulla.

85. Phryxus was the son of Athamas. Being unable to endure the ungovernable temper of his stepmother Nephele,[3] he fled and was accompanied by his sister Helle. They took with them a beautiful ram with a golden fleece, and having no ship at their command[4] they tried to cross the Hellespont seated on the animal's back.[5] Helle fell into the sea, and gave *her* name to the Hellespont: Phryxus arrived safely in Colchis at the court of Aeetes, the father of Medea. There he sacrificed the ram to Mars, and handed over his golden fleece to the king.

86. In that year also the Etrurians made preparations for war,[6] in violation of the truce. But a vast army of the Gauls, making an irruption into their territory, while their attention was diverted to another quarter,[7] made them suspend for a time the execution of their design.[8] Thereupon, relying on money, of which they had a plentiful supply,[9] they laid themselves out[10] to make the Gauls allies instead of enemies, so as to make war with the Romans with this addition to their forces.[11]

87. It was a saying of Pliny that no book was so worthless as not to be profitable in some way or other.[12]

---

[1] lived in the worst way of all.　　　[2] with great crime.
[3] Nephele, a woman of most ungovernable temper (impotentissima).
[4] cum nulla navis suppeteret.　　　[5] they sat on . . . to cross.
[6] passive.　　　[7] planning other things.
[8] diverted them for a short time from their intention.
[9] in which they had much power.　　　[10] conantur.
[11] with this army added.　　　[12] in some part.

88. At the games in the circus[1] the praetors used to present the victors with wreaths decorated with gold or silver foil, representing flowers and leaves.

89. When Xerxes was informed of the courage and also of the success of Artemisia in the sea-fight, he is said to have exclaimed (*orat. obl.*), "My women have become men, and my men women."

90. Philosophers would be very handsomely rewarded if, to use the words of Theognis, as Circe by her herbs and incantations used instantaneously to transform men into brute beasts, so they by their discourses could change brutes into men, that is to say could recall human beings, scarcely to be distinguished[2] from brute beasts, from vice to virtue, from madness to reason, from brutality to humanity. Yet philosophy can boast that at times she has effected some such result. She will quote the case of Polemo,[3] recalled by a single lecture of Xenocrates from a life of shame and from habitual profligacy[4] to soberness and austerity. But as tillage is not equally *efficacious* in all fields, so philosophy does not produce the same effect on all minds.

91. That was a fine and wise remark of Cato, that he would rather men should ask why no statue had been erected in his honour, than that they should ask why one had been erected to him. All true philosophers are of the same way of thinking.[5] They, as Aeschylus says of Amphiaraus, had rather be the best than seem to be the best. Moreover, they either refrain from seeking honours and offices, or they seek them to do good[6] to others rather than to themselves. If they obtain them they do not exult: if they are rejected they are not

---

[1] Circenses.
[2] most like.
[3] she will produce Polemo.
[4] moribus perditissimis.
[5] same mind.
[6] for the sake of the advantage.

distressed in spirit, but they bear *defeat* with calmness and moderation ; or, if they do feel aggrieved, it is for their country[1] and not for themselves.

92. A boy, who had been educated in the house of Plato, after a time went home to his father. He saw his father break out into immoderate laughter. The boy was astonished and said, "I never saw anything of this kind in the house of Plato."

93. Sulla, having taken the town of Praeneste, determined to put the whole body of the inhabitants[2] to the sword. He made an exception in favour of a man who had once been his host,[3] wishing by this act of kindness to make a return for the hospitality he had received.[4] But the man nobly refused the pardon,[5] saying, "I will not owe my life to the destroyer of my country :" and with these words he mingled with the crowd of his countrymen and was slain with them.

94. Scipio Africanus was anxious to be made consul,[6] but he saw that his friend Pompeius favoured other candidates. He therefore gave up his canvass, saying that the consulship, *even* if he obtained it, would rather be burdensome and unhallowed than honourable to him, if he won it in opposition to Pompeius.[7] He thought it better to relinquish the consulship than to lose his friend.

95. Once on a time the vulture invited the little birds to a banquet, which he proposed to give them on his birthday. When they came at the *appointed* time, he began to rend and kill them and to provide himself with a meal from the invited guests.

---

[1] rei publicae dolent vicem. [2] whatever there was of citizens.
[3] he ordered his host to be excepted. [4] imparted.
[5] *Lat.*, but he, on the other hand, nobly. . . .
[6] was eagerly seeking the consulship. [7] refragante Pompeio.

96. The shepherds had killed a sheep and were making a feast. The wolf perceiving this cried, "If I had seized on a lamb, what a stir there would be! Yet these fellows are devouring a sheep without any complaint being made."[1] Then one of the shepherds said, "*True*, for we are feasting on a sheep of our own, and not on one that belongs to another."

97. They then who say that old age has nothing to do[2] with the transaction of business, bring forward no valid argument.[3] It is much the same as[4] if they were to assert that a pilot has nothing to do with the navigation *of a ship*, since others climb the masts, others run to and fro over the decks, others work at the pumps, while he sits quiet in the stern holding the helm. His duties may[5] not be the same as those of young men : but surely they are more important and more useful.[6]

98. When Epaminondas had beaten the Spartans at Mantinea, and at the same time was conscious that he was dying from a severe wound, as soon as he recovered his senses he asked whether his shield was safe. When his weeping *attendants* told him[7] that it was safe, he asked whether the enemy was routed. When he received the answer that he desired to that question also,[8] he ordered the spear by which he had been pierced to be pulled out. So with a vast gush of blood[9] he died rejoicing and victorious.[10]

99. More elephants were killed by their drivers than by the enemy. They carried an iron spike[11] and a hammer. When the beasts became furious and began to rush

---

[1] with impunity.
[2] negant versari.
[3] bring forward nothing.
[4] similes sunt ut si qui.
[5] He may not do.
[6] better.
[7] answered.
[8] heard that also as he desired.
[9] much blood.
[10] Substantives.
[11] fabrile scalprum.

among their own *troops*, the keeper, putting *the spike*[1] between the ears just at the juncture[2] of the neck and head, drove it in with his utmost strength. This had been found to be the quickest way of despatching[3] a beast of such vast bulk, when they were past all control :[4] and Hasdrubal was the first to direct it to be done.[5]

100. When Brutus was about to enter *his* last battle, some tried to persuade[6] him not to run so great a risk : whereupon he said, "This day all will be well, or I shall care nothing about it."

---

[1] positum. [2] the joint in which the neck is united to the head.
[3] quickest way of death. [4] had overpowered hope of guiding them.
[5] iustituo. [6] abl. abs.

VOCABULARY.

Abandon, relinquo.
abide by (*keep*), sto.
ability (*to the best of my*), pro meis
    opibus.
abominable, nefarius.
about (*nearly*), ferme, fere.
absolute (*power*), regius.
abundance, copia.
abundance (*to have*), abundo.
abundance (*in*), plurimus.
abundant, uber.
accept, sumo.
accession, accessio.
accompanied by, cum.
accomplice, conscius.
accomplish, perficio, conficio.
  in accordance with, ex.
  in accordance with justice, iustus.
account, ratio.
  make no account of, negligo.
  to hand down a correct account,
    verum tradere.
accurately, vere.
accuse, accuso.
  an accused man, reus.
accustomed (*to be*), consuesco.
acquire, adipiscor, consequor, comparo.
acquit, libero.
act (*vb.*), facio.
action, factum.
act of injustice, iniuria.
  act in such a way as . . . id facio
    ut . . .
active, impiger.
actually, plane.

adamantine, adamantinus.
add, addo, adicio, adiungo.
adder, coluber.
address (*words*), facio (*verba*)
  cum . . .
adduce, profero.
admit, confiteor, fateor, concedo.
admonish, moneo.
adopt (*a plan*), capio.
adorn, decoro, orno.
advance (*vb.*), procedo, progredior.
advance (*a standard*), fero.
advanced (*in life*), aetate provectus.
advantage, utilitas, usus, lucrum,
  bonum, commodum.
  it is of advantage, conducit.
advantageous, utilis.
advice, consilium, sententia.
  to give advice, monere.
advise, suadeo (*dat.*).
advise not to do, dissuadeo.
advocate, advocatus.
affair, res.
affairs of men, res humanae.
affection, amor.
afflicted (*to be*), maereo.
afraid of (*to be*), timeo, vereor.
afterwards, deinde, postea.
again, iterum, rursus.
against, contra, adversus.
Agamemnon, onis.
age, aetas.
age (*generation*), saeculum.
agent, procurator.
agency, opera.
aggrieved (*to feel*), doleo.

agree, assentior (*dat.*), consentio de.

agree with (*fit in with*), congruo (*dat.*).

agreeable, amicus.

agreement, pactio.

aid, auxilium.

aid (*vb.*), subvenio.

akin, finitimus.

alarm, metus, timor.

alarm (*vb.*), terreo.

Alban, Albanus.

alive (*be*), supersum.

all, omnis, totus.

allow, sino, patior.

allurements, inlecebrae.

ally, socius.

almost, paene or pene, fere.

alone, solus.

already, iam,

also, etiam, quoque.

altar, ara.

alternately, alternis vicibus.

always, semper.

ambuscade, insidiae.

amuse, delecto.

amusement, delectatio.

ancestors, maiores.

anger, ira.

angry, iratus.

angry (*to be*), irascor (*dat.*).

animal, animal.

announce, nuntio.

annoy, pungo, urgueo.

annoyed (*to be*), succensco (*dat.*).

annual, annuus.

annually, quotannis.

anon, mox.

another, alius, alter.

answer (*vb.*), respondeo (*dat.*).

anxiety, cura.

any . . *that might be* . . , si quid (*gen.*) esset . .

anxious for (*to be*), cupio, aveo.

any one (*excluding all*), quisquam.

any one (*including all*), quivis, quilibet.

apart (*to be*), absum.

Apennines, Apenninus.

Apollo, inis.

apologise, utor excusatione.

apology, excusatio.

appealing to, implorans.

appearance, species.

appear in public, in publicum prodire.

appease, placo.

apple, pomum.

application (*industry*), industria.

appoint, constituo, instituo.

apprehend, comprehendo.

apprehension, metus.

approach, aditus.

approach (*vb.*), accedo ad, adeo, advento, venio ad, appropinquo.

approach (*from below*), succedo.

approve, probo, approbo.

Archias, ae, ae, am, a, a.

archery (*skill in*), ars sagittandi.

argument, argumentum.

Arion, onis.

arise, surgo.

Aristotle, Aristoteles.

arm (*vb.*), armo.

arms (*weapons*), arma.

arms (*embrace*), complexus.

army, exercitus.

arouse, excito.

arrange, instituo, statuo, dispono, colloco, paro, comparo, constituo.

arrange for, paro.

arrange in divisions, distribuo in partes.

arrangement, res, institutum.

arrive, venio, pervenio.

arrogant, arrogans.

arrow, sagitta.

art, ars.

artery, arteria.

as (*coin*), as, assis.

as often as, quotiescunque.

as soon as, quam primum, simul atque.

ashamed (*to be*), verecundor.

ask (*invite*), invito, voco.

ask, peto, rogo, interrogo.

asleep (*to be*), dormio.

ass, asinus.

assail, peto.

assault, oppugno.

assemble, congrego.
   the senate is assembling, senatus cogitur.
assembly, concio.
assign, tribuo, do, attribuo.
assist, iuvo.
assistance, auxilium, opis (*gen.*), opera, auxilium.
assistant, adiutor, minister, administer.
associate with, versor.
assuage, lenio, levo.
assurance, fides.
astrologers, Chaldaei.
astonished, admiratus.
at all, omnino.
at length, tandem.
at once, statim.
Athamas, Athamantis.
Athenians, Athenienses.
Athens, Athenae.
attack, impetus.
attack (*vb.*), invado.
attack (*vb.*) (*sickness*), afficio.
attain, pervenio.
attempt, conatus.
attend (*the senate*), esse in.
attention, opera.
attention (*in hearing*), attentio.
attentively, diligenter, attente.
attract, allicio.
augur, augur.
austerity, severitas.
authority, auctoritas.
authority (*personal*), auctor.
avail one's-self, utor.
avert, averto.
avoid, vito, fugio, abstineo.
await (*expect*), exspecto.
aware (*to be*), cognitum habeo.

Back, retro.
bad, malus, pravus.
badly, male, parum.
badly (*severely*), vehementer.
baggage, impedimenta (*pl.*).
ban (*to be under a*), interdici.
band (*of soldiers*), agmen.
banished, expulsus.

banishment, exsilium.
bank, ripa.
bankrupt (*to be*), solvendo non esse.
banquet, convivium.
banter, iocor.
barbarian, barbarus.
barren, sterilis.
bath-house, balneae.
bath-keeper, balneator.
battalion, cohors.
battering-ram, aries.
battle, proelium, pugna.
   a pitched battle, acies.
battle-array (*army in*), acies.
beach, litus.
bear, fero.
   I cannot bear, aegre fero.
beard, barba.
beast, bellua.
beast of burden, iumentum.
beat (*overcome*), supero, vinco.
beautiful, pulcher, eximius.
become, fio.
bed, lectus, cubile.
bed-chamber, cubiculum.
befall, incido (*dat.*).
beg, peto, oro, rogo.
beggar, mendicus.
begin, ordior, incipio, inchoo, instituo.
beginning, principium.
in behalf of, pro.
behold, aspicio.
believe, credo (*dat.*), confido.
belief (*in my*), quod videor mihi.
belonging to another, alienus.
beneficial, utilis.
benefit, beneficium.
   to confer a benefit, prosum.
bent, curvus.
besides, praeter.
besiege, obsido *or* obsideo.
best (*to do my*), quantum eniti possum.
bestow, largior, offero, confero.
betake, confero.
betray, prodo.
betray (*one's feelings*), indico.
better, melior.
   to be better than, vinco.

bewail, deploro, fleo de.
bid (command), iubeo, impero.
bind, obligo, vincio, obstringo.
biographies, vitae.
bird, avis.
 little bird, avicula.
birthday, dies natalis.
blame, culpa.
blame (vb.), reprehendo.
blameworthy, vituperandus.
blemish, macula.
blessed, fortunatus.
blind, caecus.
blindness, caecitas.
block up, saepio, obsido.
blockade (vb.), saepio, obsaepio.
blood-stained, cruentus.
blot, labes.
blue, caeruleus.
blunder, error.
blunt (vb.), obtundo.
boar, aper.
boast, iacto, glorior.
boat, scapha.
body, corpus.
body (marching), agmen.
Boeotians, Boeoti.
bold, audax.
bond-slave (to be a), servire servitutem.
book, liber.
booty, praeda.
borders (of country), fines.
born, natus.
both, ambo.
bough, ramus.
bound (tied), vinctus.
boundaries, fines.
bountiful, liberalis.
bow, arcus.
boy, puer.
brave, fortis.
bravely, fortiter.
break, frango.
break down (a bridge), interrumpo.
break up (a camp), moveo.
break forth, erumpo.
break in on, intervenio (*dat.*).
bribe, corrumpo (*pecunia*).
 through bribes, propter pecuniam.

bribery, ambitus.
bridge, pons.
briefly, breviter.
brilliant, praeclarus.
bring, duco, fero.
bring up, adduco.
bring up (rear), educo.
bring one's-self to think, induco.
bring under notice, adfero.
bring forward, adfero.
bring under, redigo.
bring about, efficio.
bring back, refero.
broken (fortunes), adtritus.
brother, frater.
brushwood, virgulta (*pl.*).
brutal, ferus.
brutality, immanitas.
brute beasts, ferae, pecudes.
build (a bridge), facio.
build (a city), condo.
build (a house), aedifico.
building, aedificium.
bulk, moles.
burdensome, molestus.
burn, uro, concremo.
burnt to the ground (to be), deflagrare.
bury, sepelio.
business, negotium, res.
 to have urgent business, expedio.
busy, occupatus.
but that, nisi.
buy, emo.
buy up, coemo.
buyer, emptor.

Caesar, aris.
calf, vitulus.
call, voco.
call to witness, testor.
call to mind, commemoro, recordor.
call on for advice, adhibeo ad consilium.
calmly, moderate, placate.
 with such calmness, ita moderate.
calumny, invidia.
camp, castra (*pl.*).
campaign, militia, bellum.
candidate, candidatus.

candidate, to be a, peto.
Cannae (battle of), pugna Cannensis.
canton, vicus.
canvass, petitio.
cape (headland), promontorium.
Capitol, Capitolium.
captive, captus.
capture (vb.), capio.
Capua (people of), Campani.
care, cura.
  to take care, curo.
carefully, diligenter.
carelessness, imprudentia.
carelessness (culpable), nequitia.
carriage, rheda.
carry, porto, veho, affero.
carry back, refero.
carry (a sword), habeo.
carry out, perfero, conficio.
carry on (war, etc.), gero, duco, perficio.
Carthage, Carthago, -inis.
Carthaginians, Carthaginienses, Poeni.
Carthaginian (adj.), Punicus.
case, causa.
case (statement), res.
  in my case, de me.
cast out, proicio.
cast (into prison), conicio.
cast down, deicio.
cast headlong, praecipito.
cat, feles.
catch, capio, comprehendo, prehendo.
Catiline, Catilina.
Cato, -onis.
cattle, pecus, -ŏris.
cause, causa.
cause (vb.), facio.
cause annoyance, male habere.
caution (to use), caveo.
cautiously, modice.
cavalry, eques *or* equites, equitatus.
cease, desisto, desino, finem facio.
celestial, divinus.
Celtiberians, Celtiberi.
censor, censor.
censure (vb.), reprehendo.

censurer, obiurgator.
centurion, centurio.
Ceres, -eris.
certain, certus.
certain (indefinite), quidam.
  it is certain, constat.
chain, vinculum, catena.
Chalcedonians, Chalcedonii.
chance (opportunity), facultas.
change, mutatio.
change, (vb.), muto, converto, facio ex.
characteristic (adj.), proprius.
charge, crimen.
charge (business), procuratio.
charge (exhort), hortor.
  to charge (the enemy), se offerre.
charioteer, auriga.
charm (vb.), delecto.
charming, dulcis.
chase (vb.), ago.
cheat (vb.), fallo, fraudo.
check (vb.), tardo.
cheerfully, acriter.
cherish, foveo, alo.
chest (box), arca.
chief, princeps.
chief (highest), summus.
chiefly, potissimum.
child, infans.
children, liberi.
Cicero, -onis.
citadel, arx.
citizen, civis.
city, urbs.
city (adj.), urbanus.
city-walls, moenia.
clashing, sonitus.
class, ordo.
clear, clarus.
clear (vb.), purgo.
clearly, haud dubie.
cleverly, sapienter.
climb, scando.
cloak, pallium.
close (vb.), claudo.
close to (to be), contingo.
close at hand (to be), appeto.
close (confined), arctus.
close connection, coniunctio.

cloud, nubes.
coast, ora.
Colchis, -idis.
cold, frigus.
cold (adj.), gelidus, frigidus.
colleague, collega.
collect, conduco, colligo, accio.
collect (in assembly), voco.
college, collegium.
colony, colonia.
colours (of a regiment), signa militaria.
combatant, bellator.
  non-combatant, imbellis.
come, venio.
come out, exeo.
come into vogue, inolesco.
come to life again, revivisco.
come down, degredior.
come up to, accedo ad.
command, imperium, iussum.
command (vb.), impero.
  to be in command of, duco.
commander, dux, imperator, praetor.
commence, ordior, coorior.
commencement, principium.
commend, laudo.
commit, facio, admitto.
common, communis.
commons, plebs.
communicate, communico.
community, civitas.
companion, comes.
compare, confero, comparo.
compassion (to have), misereor.
compel, cogo.
complain, queror, indignor.
complete (vb.), absolvo.
complete (a building), exstruo.
compose (plays), facio.
comprehend, intelligo.
comprehension, intelligentia.
compulsion, necessitas, vis.
comrade, commilito.
conceal, abdo, occulto, tego.
concealed, abditus.
conceive, fingo.
conceive a scheme, ineo consilium.
conclude, perficio.

condemn, damno, condemno.
condition, fortuna, status, sors.
conditions (of peace), condiciones.
  on any other condition, aliter.
  on condition that, sub ea condicione ut. . . .
conduct (vb.), duco.
confer (bestow), affero, dono.
conference, colloquium.
confidence, fides.
confidence (to have), credo (dat.).
confidently, audacter.
confine, includo.
congratulate, gratulor (dat.).
conquer, vinco, subigo, -egi.
conscience, conscientia.
conscious of (to be), video.
consider (weigh), delibero, consulto, discepto.
consider (think), arbitror, puto, cogito.
considerable time, aliquamdiu.
consolation, solatium, consolatio.
conspicuous (to become), inclaresco.
constant, continuus.
constantly, assidue, semper, saepe.
constellation, astrum.
constraint, necessitas.
construct, struo.
construct (a road, camp, etc.), munio, facio.
consul, consul.
consular, consularis.
consulship, consulatus.
consult, consulo.
consult for (seek), quaero.
consultation, consultatio.
consummate, summus.
contagion, contagio.
contain, habeo.
contemporary, aequalis.
contempt (treat with), contemno.
content it should be so, id patior facile.
contest, certamen.
contest (vb.), contendo.
contract (vb.), iungo.
conveniently, commode.
conversation, sermo.
converse (vb.), colloquor.

convey (corn), subveho.
convict, condemno.
convict (prove wrong), convinco.
copy, exemplum.
Corinth, Corinthus.
Corinthians, Corinthii.
corn, frumentum.
corpse, cadaver.
corrupt, corruptus.
couch, lectus.
counsel, consilium.
count, computo.
countenance, vultus.
country (native), patria.
country (state), res publica.
country (district), ager.
 fellow-countrymen, cives, popu-
  lares.
 in the country, ruri.
country-districts, agri.
courage, virtus.
courageous, fortis.
course, cursus.
course of nature, ordo naturalis.
court (of justice), iudicium.
court (pay attention to), colo.
courtesy, humanitas, comitas.
cover (vb.), operio.
covered (with ships), constratus.
covetousness, avaritia.
cow, vacca.
coward, ignavus, timidus.
cowardly (adj.), ignavus.
cowardice, ignavia.
crabbed, morosus.
crane, grus.
craft, calliditas.
creature, animal.
credible, credibilis.
creditable (to be), esse honori, glorio-
 sus.
creep, serpo.
crestfallen, humilis.
crime, scelus, facinus, flagitium.
crisis, tempestas.
cross (vb.), traicio, -ieci, transmitto,
 transeo.
crops, fruges.
crowd, turba.
crowd of visitors, celebritas.

crowded, refertus.
crucify, in crucem sufferre.
cruel, crudelis.
cruelly, crudeliter.
crush, opprimo, elido.
cry out, clamo, clamito.
Ctesiphon, -ontis.
cultivate, colo.
cunning, calliditas.
current, flumen.
custom, mos, consuetudo.
cut, seco.
cut hair or beard, tondeo.
cut off, suffero, excipio.
cut off (by interdict), interdico.
cut down, caedo, interficio.
cut one's way through, excido.

Daily, cotidianus.
dance (vb.), salto.
danger, periculum, discrimen.
dangerous (disease), gravior.
dare, audeo.
daring, audacia.
dark saying, ambage (abl.).
darkness, tenebrae.
dart, iaculum, telum.
dash in, irruo, irrumpo.
dated (as a letter), datus.
daughter, filia.
day, dies.
day and night, noctes diesque.
 in the days when . . . iisdem
  temporibus, quibus. . . .
day is breaking, lucere caepit.
daybreak, lux.
 about daybreak, sub lucem.
 at daybreak, prima luce.
 with the dawn of day, prima luce.
daylight, lux.
 in the daytime, interdiu.
dead man, mortuus.
deaf, surdus.
 somewhat deaf, surdaster.
deal kindly, benigne facio.
dear, carus.
dearth, inopia frugum.
 time of dearth, caritas.
death, nex, mors, interitus.
debar, impedio.

debauchery, luxuria.
deceitful, fallax.
deceitfulness, fraus.
deceive, decipio, fallo.
deception, furtum.
decide, decerno.
decision, arbitrium, iudicium.
   come to a decision, decerno.
deck (*vb.*), orno.
decks, fori.
declare (*war*), indīco.
declare (*intention*), ostendo.
decline (*refuse*), recuso.
decorate, orno, decoro.
decorated, insignis.
decree, decretum.
deed, factum.
deem, iudico.
deep, altus.
defence, praesidium.
   in defence of, pro.
defend, defendo, tutor, protego.
defender, defensor.
defer, differo.
deficient (*to be*), desum.
defile (*vb.*), polluo.
degradation, infamia.
degrading, turpis, informis.
delay, mora.
   to delay in departing, tardius proficisci.
delight, voluptas.
delightful, iucundus.
deliver up, trado.
Delphi, Delphi (*pl.*).
demand (*vb.*), posco.
deny, nego.
depart, discedo, abscedo, proficiscor.
departure, discessus.
depend, pendeo.
deposited (*to be*), inesse.
depreciate, minuo.
deprive, privo.
   to be deprived of, careo.
derive, capio, haurio.
describe (*in detail*), expono.
describe (*in writing*), scribo.
desert (*vb.*), desero.
deserter, perfuga.

deserve, mereor.
design, consilium.
design (*vb.*), volo.
desire, studium, cupiditas, voluntas.
desire (*vb.*), opto, cupio, volo.
   more to be desired, potior.
despair (*vb.*), despero.
despise, sperno, contemno.
desponding, abiectus.
destiny, fatum.
destroy, deleo, aboleo.
destroyer, exstinctor.
detach, avoco.
deter, deterreo.
determine, instituo, decerno.
devoid, expers.
devoid of (*to be*), vaco.
devote, voveo, devoveo, offero.
devote (*to give*), do.
devoted, deditus.
devour, comedo.
dictator, dictator.
die, morior, mortem obeo, exanimor.
die (emphatic), emorior.
differ from, dissentio cum.
difference, diversitas.
difficulty, difficultas.
   with difficulty, aegre.
diffuse (*vb.*), diffundo, distribuo.
dignity, maiestas.
dignity (*of a man*), dignitas.
diligence, industria, diligentia.
dinner, cena.
direct, rego, dirigo, moderor, praecipio, instituo.
direction (*command*), mandatum.
disappoint, fallo.
disaster, calamitas.
   with disastrous results, magna cum clade.
discipline, disciplina.
discover, invenio.
discoverer, inventor.
discreet, modestus.
discussion, disceptatio.
disdain (*vb.*), dedignor.
disease, morbus.
disgrace, turpitudo, ignominia, dedecus.

disgraceful, turpis.
disgracefully, flagitiose.
disgusting, foedus.
dishonest, turpis.
dismal, tristis.
dismiss, dimitto.
disposition, indoles, natura, ingenium.
dispute, discordia, controversia.
disquietude, sollicitudo.
distance (at a), procul.
distant (to be), absum.
distinguish, distinguo.
distress, miseriae (*pl.*).
distress (vb.), fatigo.
distressed (to be), angor.
distressing, gravis.
disturbance, dissensio.
disturbed, perturbatus.
ditch, fossa.
divert (turn away), averto.
divide, divido, distribuo.
divination, divinatio.
divine, divinus.
do, facio, ago, gero.
do you mean to say? numne?
dog, canis.
dolphin, delphinus.
domestic economy, tueri rem familiarem.
dominant (to be), dominor.
door, ianua, fores, ostium.
   at the door, ab ostio.
double (a cape), flecto.
doubt (vb.), dubito.
   no doubt, certe, sane.
   I doubt whether, nescio an.
   I cannot doubt, mihi non est dubium.
doubtful, obscurus, dubius.
doubtless, nimirum.
downcast, perculsus.
drag, traho.
draught, haustus.
draw, traho.
draw water, haurio.
draw (furrow), duco.
draw (up army), instruo.
draw back, recipio.
draw off, detraho.

draw near, prope accedo.
dread (vb.), timeo, metuo, pertimesco.
dream, somnium.
dress, vestis, cultus.
dress (a wound), foveo.
drink, potio.
drink (vb.), bibo, poto.
drive, ago, pello.
drive ashore, defero.
drive (banish), eicio.
drive in, adigo.
drive out, eicio.
driver, rector.
drop, gutta.
drop (give up), omitto.
drought, siccitas.
drowned at sea, perire in mari.
Druids, Druides.
due (to be), deberi.
duty, officium.
dwell in, incolo, habeo.
dwell on (a subject), commoror.
dwell (live), vivo.

Each, singuli.
eager, avidus.
eager for, studiosus.
   to be eager, gestio, aveo.
eagerly, avide, ambitiose.
eagle, aquila.
ear, auris.
earnest desire, studium.
earnestness, contentio, studium.
earth, terra.
earth-work, agger.
earthquake, terrae motus.
ease, otium.
   to enjoy one's ease, otiosus esse.
easy, facilis.
easy (life, in), securus.
   at ease, otiosus.
eclipse, defectio.
   to be eclipsed, deficere.
educate, educo.
effect (vb.), efficio.
effeminate, mollis.
egg, ovum.
Egypt, Aegyptus.
Egyptians, Aegyptii.

elder (*brother*), maior.
elect (*consul, dictator*), creo.
elephant, elephantus.
elm, ulmus.
eloquence, eloquentia.
eloquent, disertus, eloquens.
embalm, condio.
embassy, legatio.
embellish, polio.
embezzlement, peculatus.
embrace, amplexus.
embrace (*vb.*), complector.
eminent, illustris, singularis.
emotions, motus (*pl.*).
Emperor, Princeps, Imperator.
empire, imperium.
employ, adhibeo, utor.
employment, negotium.
encamp, castra pono.
encourage, hortor.
end, finis, exitus, summa.
end (*death*), exitus.
end of street, ultima platea.
endure, fero, patior.
enemy (*personal*), inimicus.
enemy (*public*), hostis.
engage (*in battle*), committere proelium.
engage in (*business*), ago.
   to be engaged in, versor.
   to commence an engagement, committere proelium.
enjoy, fruor, oblecto me.
enjoyment, voluptas.
enormously, plurimum.
enough, satis.
enrich, augeo.
enter, intro, ingredior.
entertained, exceptus.
entertainer, convivator.
enthusiasm, spiritus, ira.
   to be enthusiastic, ardeo.
entice, elicio, perpello.
entire, totus.
entirely, omnino.
entreaties, preces.
entrust, committo.
envious (*to be*), invideo (*dat.*).
envoy, lēgatus.
envy, invidia.

envy (*vb.*), invideo (*dat.*).
Epaminondas, -ae -ae -am.
Ephesian, Ephesius.
equal, par.
equally, peraeque, iuxta.
equanimity (*with*), facile.
equestrian, equester.
equip, armo, instruo.
equity, aequitas.
eradicate, depello.
erect, erigo.
erect (*a statue*), pono.
Erechtheus, -ei.
escape, effugio, elabor.
escape by concealment, lateo.
escape by flight, fugio.
essential, necessarius.
estate (*property*), possessio.
esteem, diligo, -lexi.
Etrurians, Etrusci, Tusci.
even, etiam.
evening (*towards*), sub vesperum.
evening (*in the*), vesperi.
event, res.
ever (*always*), semper.
ever (*at any time*), unquam.
evil, malus.
exact (*vb.*), sumo.
exactly the same distance, tantumdem viae.
example, exemplum.
exceedingly, valde, admodum.
excellence, laus.
excellent, optimus.
except, nisi, praeter.
except (*vb.*), excipio.
excessive, nimius.
excite, moveo.
excitement, excitatio, concitatio.
excuse, venia.
exhaust, conficio.
exhaustion, lassitudo.
exhibit (*a play*), do.
exhort, hortor.
exhortation, hortatus.
exist, sum.
expect, spero, exspecto.
expectation, exspectatio, spes.
expediency, utilitas.
expedient, utilis.

expense, sumtus.
experience, usus.
experienced, peritus.
expiate, luo.
explain, expono.
explanation, ratio.
expose, oppono.
extend, pateo.
extent (to some), aliqua parte.
extortion, res repetundae.
extraordinary, maximus.
extravagance, luxus.
extremely, valde, vehementer.
extremely vexed (to be), moleste fero.
exult, exsulto.
eye, oculus.
eyesight, lumina oculorum.
before one's eyes, in conspectu.
eye-witness, qui vidit.

Fable, fabula.
face, ōs, oris ; facies, vultus.
face (vb.), oppeto.
facing, contra, adversus.
fail, deficio, desum.
fail to find, desidero.
fair, pulcher.
fair (wind), secundissimus.
faith, fides.
faithful, fidelis.
Falernian, Falernus.
fall (vb.), cado, occido, concido, iaceo.
fall into, incido.
fall (as a building), ruo.
fall (in a heap), corruo.
fall (be slain), interficior.
fall off, decido.
fall down, decido.
fall, occasus.
fallow (to lie), quiesco, quievi.
false, falsus.
fame, gloria.
family, familia.
famine, fames.
famous, celeber, nobilis.
far, longe.
farm, fundus.
farmer, agricola.
farm-labourer, agrestis.

fashion, ritus, modus.
fashion (vb.), fabricor.
fate, fatum.
father, pater.
father-in-law, socer.
fault, culpa, delictum.
favour, gratia.
favour (vb.), faveo (dat.).
this is in favour of . . ., hoc facit a . . .
favours, beneficium.
favourable, bonus.
favourably, benigne.
less favourable, iniquus.
fear, timor, metus.
fear (vb.), timeo, metuo, vereor, paveo.
to be somewhat fearful, subvereor.
feast on, epulor (abl.).
fee, merces.
feed, alo.
feel, fero, sentio.
feeling, sensus.
fellow (as term of contempt), homo.
fellow-soldier, commilito.
fellowship, societas.
fertile, fertilis, uber.
fertility, ubertas.
fetch, arcesso.
few, pauci.
very few, perpauci.
a few, aliquot.
only a few, pauci.
fickleness, inconstantia.
fidelity, fides.
field, ager, campus.
fierce, acer.
fight, pugna, proelium, certamen.
fight (vb.), pugno, armis contendo.
fight it out, decerto.
fill, repleo, compleo, impleo.
find, invenio, reperio.
find (catch), offendo.
find (obtain), nanciscor.
find fault with, accuso, culpo.
find (pleasure in), capio.
finger, digitus.
finish, perficio, conficio.
finished, perfectus, confectus.

finisher, confector.
fire, ignis, flamma.
fire (to be on), ardeo.
firm, firmus.
first rank (of), in primis.
first-rate, optimus.
fish, piscis.
fit, idoneus.
fix, constituo.
fixed, certus, status.
flank, latus.
flash (vb.), mico.
flatter, adulor.
flee, fugio, profugio.
flee for refuge, confugio.
fleece, vellus.
fleet, classis.
flight, fuga.
   put to flight, vertere in fugam.
fling, proicio.
flit away, praetervolo.
flogged to death (to be), caedi virgis.
flogging, verbera (*pl.*)
flourish, exsto, vigeo.
flourishing, florens.
flow, fluo.
flow (of eloquence), copia.
flower, flos.
fly (vb.), volo.
fly away, avolo, evolo.
foil (thin metal), bractea.
folding-doors, valvae.
follow, sequor, insequor.
follow close, subsequor.
following (day), posterus.
folly, stultitia.
follies, ineptiae.
   downright folly, dementia, amentia.
fond, amans.
food, cibus, pastus, victus.
foolish, stultus.
foot, pes.
foot-soldier, pedes.
forage (vb.), praedor.
forbid, veto.
force, vis.
force (vb.), cogo.
forebode, portendo.

forecast (to make), spes iacio.
forefathers, maiores.
foresee (future events), praesentio.
forest, silva.
foretell, dico futurum, praedico.
forget, obliviscor.
forgive, do veniam.
forgiveness, venia.
form (a league), iungo.
form a scheme, cogito, ineo consilium.
form societies, congregor.
formidable, gravis.
forsake, desero, dimitto, relinquo.
fort, castellum, castrum.
fortify, munio, permunio.
fortune, fortuna.
foul, nefarius, foedus.
found (a city), condo.
founded, conditus, constitutus.
founder (of a sect), inventor.
founder (of a city), conditor.
fox, vulpes.
frankly, aperte.
fray, certamen.
free, liber.
free from taxes, immunis.
free from (to be), vaco.
freely (of your own free will), vestrapte sponte.
freely (without restraint), libere.
freedman, libertus.
freedom, libertas.
freedom of city, ius civitatis.
fresh, novus, recens.
friend, amicus.
   no friend to, inimicus.
friendly, amice.
friendship, amicitia, societas.
friendship of the great, insignes amicitiae.
frighten, terreo.
   in front of, ante, ante frontem.
frontier, fines (*pl.*).
full, plenus.
   to be full of vigour, vigeo.
   to be full of life, vivo.
fully, satis.
funeral pile, rogus.
furnish (afford), praebeo.

furrow, sulcus.
further (adj.), reliquus.
further (on the other side), ulterior.
   on the further side, trans.
further (to a greater extent), latius.
furthest extremity, extremus.

Gabii, Gabii (*pl.*).
gain, emolumentum, lucrum.
gain a title, appellor, nomen invenio.
games (public), ludi.
garden, hortus.
   pleasure gardens, horti.
garland, corona.
garrison, praesidium.
garrulous, loquax.
gate, porta.
gather, carpo, lĕgo.
Gaul, Gallia.
   a Gaul, Gallus.
general, dux, imperator.
generation (an age), saeculum.
generous, liberalis.
genius, ingenium.
gentleman, homo ingenuus.
Germans, Germani.
get rid of, depono.
get sight of, conspicio, -spexi.
get over, transeo.
giant, gigas.
gift, donum, munus.
girl, puella.
give, do, reddo.
give (afford), praebeo.
give back, reddo.
give good advice, bona praecipio.
give up (hand over), trado, do, dedo.
give up (cease), desino.
give up (a project), desto a.
give way, decedo, parco, cedo.
glad (to be), gaudeo.
gladly, libenter *or* lubenter.
gloomy, tristis.
glorious, magnificus.
glorious deeds, virtutes.
go, eo, venio.
go away, discedo, abeo.

go back, redeo.
go down, descendo.
go on, pergo.
go out, procedo.
go out (in public), prodeo.
go under, subeo.
God, Deus.
goddess, dea.
gold, aurum.
golden, aureus.
good, bonus.
good-will, voluntas.
good-feeling, benevolentia.
good-for-nothing, nequam.
   a good education, eruditio.
govern, rego, guberno, administro.
government, imperium.
gradually, sensim.
grammar-school, ludus litterarius.
grandfather, avus.
grant (vb.), do, concedo.
   to grant permission, facere potestatem.
grass, herba, gramen.
grateful, gratus.
grateful (to be), gratias habere.
   to express one's gratitude, agere gratias.
gravity, severitas.
great, magnus.
great-grandfather, proavus.
Grecian (adj.), Graecus.
Greece, Graecia.
Greek (adj.), Graecus.
green, viridis.
   to be green, vireo.
   to become green, vireo, viresco.
grief, dolor, luctus, maeror.
ground, humus.
   on the ground, humi.
grove, lucus, nemus.
grow-old, senesco.
grudge, parco (*dat.*).
guard, custos, praesidium.
guard (vb.), custodio.
   off one's guard, imprudens.
guest (at a dinner), conviva.
guest (staying), hospes.
guide (vb.), duco, rego.
guilty, nocens.

Habit, usus, consuetudo.
habits, mores.
habitual, inveteratus.
Hades, inferi (*pl.*).
hail (*vb.*) saluto.
hair, capillus, coma.
half, dimidium.
half-way up, medius.
hammer, malleus.
hand, manus.
  to be at hand, insto.
hand (*a letter, etc.*), reddo.
hand over, trado.
handmaid, ancilla.
hanged (*to be*), suspendor.
Hannibal, -balis.
happen (*as a matter of course*), fio.
happen (*as a matter of accident*),
  accido.
happily, iucunde, bene.
happy, beatus.
harass, vexo.
harbour, portus.
hard, durus, difficilis.
hard-hearted, crudelis.
hard pressed (*to be*), urgeor.
hard to please, difficilis.
hare, lepus.
harm, incommodum.
harmony, concordia.
  to be in harmony with each other
    (inter se concinere).
harry, perdo.
haste (*in*), confestim.
hate (*vb.*), odi.
haughty, superbus.
have, habeo.
have (*possess*), possideo.
have in hand, ago.
head, caput.
head above water (*to have*), cum
  capite exstare ex aqua.
  to be at the head of affairs, praesum.
heal, sano.
health, valetudo, salus.
  in good health, salvus.
healthy, saluber.
  to be healthy, corpore valeo.
  to keep in good health, valeo.
hear, audio.

heart, cor.
heart of country, interiora.
heat, calor, ardor.
height, altitudo.
heir, heres.
Helen, Helena.
Helle, -es, -e, -en, -e, -e.
Hellespont, Hellespontus.
helm, clavus.
help, auxilium.
help (*vb.*), iuvo.
hem in, intercludo.
herald, praeco.
herb, herba.
here, hic.
hereafter, postea.
Hesiod, Hesiodus.
hesitate, dubito, cunctor.
hesitation, cunctatio.
hidden, occultus.
hide, abdo, occulto, tego.
high, altus.
high order (*of a*), excellens.
high regard for (*to have a*), diligo.
high treason, maiestas.
higher (*in rank*), superior.
highly, vehementer, valde.
hill, collis, mons.
hinder, obsto.
hire, conduco.
history, historia.
hit, ferio (*perf.* percussi).
hold, teneo, obtineo.
hold (*an oration*), habeo.
hold (*a levy*), habeo.
hold (*an office*), gero.
hold (*as a conviction*), censeo.
hold fast, persevero in.
hold supreme sway, dominor.
hold out (*offer*), propono.
home, domus.
  at home, domi.
Homer, Homerus.
honest, integer, bonus.
  to be honest, recte facio.
honestly, honeste.
honesty, integritas.
honorable, honestus, amplus, gloriae
  esse.
  most honorably, summa fide.

honour, fides, integritas.
honour (*rank* or *position*), dignitas.
hope, spes.
hope (*vb.*), spero, opto.
hopeful (*to be*), spero.
hopeless (*not to be hoped for*), desperatus.
horn, cornu.
horse, equus.
horseman, eques.
hospitality, hospitium.
host, hospes.
host (*of men*), acies.
host (*vast number*), multitudo.
hostage, obses.
hostile, inimicus.
  in hostile fashion, hostiliter.
house, domus, aedes (*pl.*).
how, qui, quomodo.
how great, quantus.
how can I help? Quidni?
human, humanus.
human sacrifices, homines pro victimis.
humanity, humanitas.
humble, humilis.
humbly, summisse, suppliciter.
hunger, fames.
hurry, irruo.
hurry up, accelero.
hurt, offendo, laedo.
husband, vir, maritus, coniunx.
husbandman, agricola.

I for my part, equidem.
I indeed, equidem.
idle, nihil agens.
idleness, ignavia.
ignorance, inscitia, ignoratio.
ignorant, imperitus, ignarus, expers.
ignorant (*to be*), nescio, ignoro, ignarus sum.
ill (*to be*), laboro.
imitate, imitor.
immense, maximus.
immensely, maxime, vehementer, plurimum.
immoderately (*without restraint*), effuse.

immoderately (*excessively*), praeter modum.
immortality, immortalitas.
impair, minuo.
impart, communico.
impiety, impietas.
impious, impius.
implant, insero.
important, magnus, gravis.
  to be so important, esse tanti.
  to think of more importance, praefero.
imported, peregrinus.
importunate, improbus.
impregnable, inexpugnabilis.
impudence, audacia.
impudent, impudens.
impunity (*with*), impune.
incantation, cantus.
include (*embrace*), complector.
inconsistent (*to be*), pugnare inter se.
inconvenient (*to be*), incommodo.
increase (*vb., grow*), cresco, accresco.
increase (*make to grow*), augeo.
increasing (*adj.*), maior.
Indian (*an*), ex Indis quidam.
indicate, indicio esse.
indifferent character (*of*), minus probatus.
indignation, dolor.
indisputable, non dubius.
induce, impetro ut, perpello, persuadeo.
induce to believe, persuadeo.
industry, industria.
infamous, nefarius.
infantry, pedes *or* pedites.
inflict, infero, impono.
influence, auctoritas, opes, vis.
influence (*with a person*), gratia.
  to have influence, valeo.
  to have so much influence, tantum posse.
inform, certiorem facio, nuntio (*dat.*).
infuse (*courage*), addo.
inhabit, incolo.
inhabitant, incola.
injunction, praeceptum.
injure, noceo (*dat.*).

injury, malum.
injustice, iniuria, iniustitia.
  act of injustice, iniuria.
inner, interior.
innocent, innocens.
inscription, epigramma.
  to have an inscription, inscribi.
insolence, contumacia.
insolvent (to be), solvendo non esse.
inspect, inspicio.
instantaneously, statim.
instruct, doceo, instruo.
instructor, magister.
integrity, integritas.
intellect, mens.
  the intelligible, quae percipi possunt.
intend to (do, etc.), *fut. part.*, *or*, cogito.
intention, voluntas, mens, animus, propositum.
intercourse, congressio.
intercourse (to have), versor.
interest, commodum.
intermarriage, connubium.
interment, sepultura.
interrupted (to be), intermitti.
intervene (to let a day), diem intermitto.
interview, colloquium.
intimacy, consuetudo.
intimate friend, familiaris.
intoxicated, ebrius.
intrenchments, munitiones.
introduce, introduco, induco.
invite, voco, invito.
iron, ferrum.
irruption (make an), ingredior.
island, insula.
issue, eventus.
Italy, Italia.

Jest (vb.), iocor.
Jew, Iudaeus.
join, coniungo.
journey, iter.
joy, laetitia.
joyful, laetus.
judge, iudex.
judge (vb.), iudico.

judgment, iudicium.
judgment (good sense), consilium.
junction (of waters), confluens.
Juno, Iuno, -nonis.
Jupiter, Iuppiter, Iovis.
just, iustus.
  perfectly just, iustissimus.
just (now), modo.
justice, iustitia.

Keep, *(preserve, retain)*, servo, retineo, conservo.
keep (continue), maneo, se tenere.
keep (restrain), habeo.
keep (preserve), servo.
keep (one's word), in fide stare.
keep (an account), habeo.
keep in check, coerceo, teneo.
keep under command, rego, impero.
keep under control, domitum habeo.
keep watch, excubo.
keep guard, custodio.
keep up, tueor.
keeper, magister.
key, clavis.
kill, neco, occido.
kind, bonus.
  to be kind to, foveo.
kind (sort), genus.
  nothing of this kind, nihil tale.
kindly, amice.
kindness (act of), beneficium.
king, rex.
  like a king, regaliter.
kingly-power, regnum.
  to have kingly power, regnare.
  to exercise kingly power, regnum obtinere.
knife, culter.
knight, eques.
knot, nodus.
know, nosco *(perf.* novi), cognosco, scio.
  not knowing, insciens.
know of, cognosco.
  to know more than . . . doctior esse.
knowledge, notitia, scientia.
known, cognitus.

Labour, labor.
labourers (*on a farm*), cultores agri.
lad, puer.
lair, cubile.
lamb, agnus.
lame, claudus.
lament, lugeo, maereo, doleo.
land, terra.
land (*cultivated*), ager.
land a fleet, classem appellere.
language (*as Greek*), litterae.
large, magnus, ingens.
last (*vb.*), duro.
lasting, diuturnus.
late (*adv.*), sero.
late in the day, multum diei.
lately, nuper.
laugh (*vb.*), rideo.
laugh at, rideo.
laughable, ridiculus.
laughing-stock, ludibrium.
law (*statute*), lex.
  to make a law, ferre legem.
law (*in general*), ius.
lawfully, iure.
lay (*put on*), impono.
lay before, defero.
lay down, depono.
lay in (*corn*), provideo.
lay violent hands on, admovere manus.
lay waste, vasto.
laziness, desidia, pigritia.
lazy, piger.
lead (*metal*), plumbum.
lead (*vb.*), duco.
lead away, abduco.
lead back, reduco.
lead forth, educo.
lead into (*danger*), deduco.
lead on, adduco.
leader, dux.
leaf, folium, frons.
league, societas.
leap down, desilio.
leap on, insilio.
learn, disco.
learn (*find out*), cognosco.
learned, doctus, eruditus.
learning, doctrina.

leave, relinquo, linquo, discedo, exeo, excedo.
lecture, disputatio.
left (*remaining*), reliquus.
left (*direction*), sinister.
legally, legibus.
legion, legio.
leisure, otium.
  to be at leisure, vaco, otiosus sum.
length (*at*), aliquando.
let an opportunity pass, praetermitto.
let slip, dimitto.
letter, litterae, epistula.
levy, delectus.
liar, mendax.
lick, lambo.
lid, operculum.
lie, iaceo.
lie dormant, iaceo.
lie hidden, lateo.
lieutenant, legatus.
life, vita, anima, caput.
light, lux.
lighted, luminosus.
lightly, strictim.
like (*vb.*), amo.
like (*adj.*), similis.
likeness, similitudo.
lily, lilium.
limit, terminus.
limp, claudico.
line of march, iter.
lineaments, lineamenta.
lips (*on one's*), in ore.
listen, audio.
literature, litterae.
little, parvus.
little (*but*), parum.
little-child, infans.
little way (*a*), paullulum.
live, vivo.
live an idle life, in otio vivere.
loan (*on*), mutuus.
Locri, Locri (*pl.*).
log, lignum.
long ago, iampridem.
  any longer, diutius.
long for, appeto.
longing (*adj.*), avidus.

longing, aviditas, spes.
look (countenance), vultus.
look for, quaero, requiro.
look for (expect), exspecto.
lord, dominus.
lose, amitto, perdo.
loss, damnum, fraus, iactura.
lore, amor.
love (vb.), amo, diligo.
low, humilis.
   in a low voice, summisse.
lurk, lateo.
lust, cupiditas.
luxuriant (to be), vireo.
luxury, luxus.

Macedonian, a, Macedo, -onis.
machinations, insidiae.
madness, dementia.
magistrate, magistratus.
magnet, magnes, -etis.
maiden, virgo, puella.
maintain, tueor.
maintain (an argument), defendo.
maintain (feed), alo.
make, facio, struo.
make (a dictator), creo.
make (a feast), celebro.
make (turn out), evado.
make a return, penso gratiam.
make a stand, obsto, offero me.
make a suggestion, subicio.
make for (seek), peto.
make one's way, dirigo iter, peto.
make out, cognitum habeo, compertum habeo.
make unfair profit, praedor.
make up (complete), conficio.
make up one's mind, constituo, decerno.
make war, bello.
make way, evado.
man, homo, vir.
man of experience, doctus.
man of mark, praestans, optimus.
manage, gero.
manifest (to make), declarare.
manifest (to be), pateo.
mantle, amiculum.
manufactory, officina.

many, multus.
many men, plerique.
march, agmen, iter.
mark (men of), optimi.
mark (vb.), video.
marriage, matrimonium.
marriage-portion, dos.
   to give in marriage, dare in matrimonium, collocare.
marry (a wife), duco.
   to be married to (a husband), nubo.
marshal (vb.), instruo.
mast (of ship), malus.
master (vb.), vinco, supero.
master (a subject), perdisco.
master, magister, dominus, herus.
mastery, (get the), superior esse.
matter, negotium, res.
meadow, pratum.
meal, epulae.
means, modus.
meanwhile, interim, interea.
measure (vb.), metior.
meditate, meditor, cogito.
meet, occurro.
meet (come together), convenio.
meeting, adj., obvius (dat.).
melodious, dulcis.
memory, memoria.
men (soldiers), milites.
mention (vb.), dico, memoro.
merit, virtus.
messenger, nuntius.
method, via.
mid, medius.
   in the midst of, inter.
mien, species.
might, vires.
Miletus (belonging to), Milesius.
mind (take care), caveo.
mine (in a siege), cuniculus.
mingle, admiscere se.
minister of justice, magistratus.
minutely, accurate.
miser, avarus.
miserably, foede.
misfortune, dolor, calamitas, malum.
miss a mark, aberro.

missile, telum.
mist, nebula.
mistake, error, erratum.
   to be greatly mistaken, magno in
     errore versari.
moderate, modicus.
moderately, mediocriter.
moderation, moderatio.
   with moderation, moderate.
money, pecunia.
monument (proof), exemplar.
moon, luna.
morality, virtus.
morning (in the,) mane.
Moselle, Mosa.
moss, muscus.
most of, plerique.
mother, mater.
mother-in-law, socrus.
   stepmother, noverca.
motive, causa.
mountain, mons.
mourn, gemo.
move, moveo.
move on a place, admoveo.
much, multus.
murder (vb)., interficio.
murder, interitus.
murmur (vb.), fremo.
mutiny, seditio.

Naked, nudus.
name, nomen.
name (appoint), dico.
   give a name to, nomino, appello.
named (declared), editus.
narrate, narro.
narrow, angustus.
narrow-pass, angustiae.
nation, gens.
native-city, patria.
natural philosopher, physicus.
nature, natura, natura rerum.
navigate, navigo.
navigators, qui navigant.
near, iuxta.
nearest, proximus.
nearness, propinquitas.
necessity, necessitas.

neck, collum.
neck (back of), cervix.
need (vb.), egeo, opus est.
neglect, (vb.), negligo.
neighbouring, vicinus, finitimus.
neither, nec, neque.
neither, (adj.), neuter.
   on neither side, non utraque
     parte.
Nephele, -es, -e, -en, -e, -e.
Nero,-onis.
nervous (timid), timidus.
net, rete.
never, nunquam.
new, novus.
Nicopolis, -is, -i, -im.
night, nox.
   at night-fall, nocte prima.
no one, nemo.
nobility, nobilitas.
nobly, libere, honeste, cum
   magna virtute.
nobody, nemo.
noon, meridies.
not, non, ne.
not a whit, nihilo.
not at all, minime.
notable, memorabilis.
notary, scriba.
nothing, nihil.
notorious, famosus.
nourish, alo.
now, nunc, iam.
now-a-days, quotidie.
number, numerus.
numbers, multitudo.
numerous, multus.
nut, nux.

Oar, remus.
oath, iusiurandum.
   to take an oath, iuro.
obey, pareo, obedio ; (dat.).
obliging-disposition, voluntas.
oblivion, oblivio.
obscure, obscurus.
obscurity, obscuritas.
observe (mentally), animadverto,
   animum adverto.

observe (*physically*), conspicio, viso, noto.
obtain, impetro, adipiscor, obtineo.
obtain relief, solvor.
occupations, res.
occupied, occupatus, implicatus.
occupy, teneo, occupo, obtineo.
ocean, mare.
odious, turpissimus.
odium, invidia.
offence, peccatum.
offend, offendo.
offer, offero, defero.
offer (*promise*), polliceor.
offer sacrifice, sacrifico.
offered, datus.
office, magistratus, honos.
often, saepe.
olive (*tree or fruit*), olea.
olive-plantation, olea.
old, antiquus, vetus.
old age, senectus.
old man, senex.
Olympian, Olympius.
Olympias, -adis.
Olympic games, Olympia (*pl.*).
omen, omen.
one, unus.
one (*of two*), alter.
one—another, alius—alius.
   at one time, aliquando.
only (*one place*), omnino.
   not only . . . non modo. . . .
open (*vb.*), aperio.
open (*to be*), pateo.
   in the open fields, in agro.
openly, palam, aperte.
opinion, opinio.
opinion of a senator, sententia.
opportunity, facultas.
   as opportunities arise, per occasiones.
oppose (*an argument*), oppugnare.
opposed to, inimicus.
opposite, contrarius, adversus.
oracle, oraculum.
orator, orator.
oratorical, oratoricus.
oratorical power, eloquentia.
oratory, oratio, or gerund of dico.

order, ordo.
   in order, ordine.
order (*vb.*), iubeo.
order to furnish, impero.
ordinances (*to make*), statuo.
originate with, orior.
ornament, ornamentum.
otherwise, aliter.
otherwise than, contra quam.
Otho, -onis.
outlet, exitus.
over, super, supra.
over (*across*), trans.
overpower, opprimo, vinco.
overpowering, tantus.
ox, bos.

Pacify, lenio.
page (*of a letter*), pagina.
pain, dolor.
   to take pains, do operam, pro-video.
painstaking, diligens.
paint, pingo.
painter, pictor.
pang, dolor.
panic, formido.
pardon, venia.
pardon (*vb.*), ignosco (*dat.*).
parricide (*act of*), parricidium.
part, pars.
   for the most part, maxime.
part (*to take*) *in*, intersum.
part (*to take*) *with*, facio cum.
partaking, particeps.
participator, particeps.
particular (*in*), imprimis.
   in every particular, omni ex parte.
particular (*individual*), singulus.
partner, socius.
parts (*ability*), ingenium.
pass (*in hills*), saltus.
pass (*vb.*), iter facio.
pass (*spend*), ago, dego.
pass a law, ferre legem.
pass away, intereo, transeo, effugio.
pass over, praetereo.

passage (in a book), locus.
passion, iracundia, ira.
passionate desire, cupiditas.
passions, cupiditates, libidines.
past, praeteritus.
patient, patiens.
patron, patronus.
pay, pretium.
pay (vb.), luo, pendo, solvo.
pay a visit to, venio ad, viso.
pay the penalty, do poenas, luo poenas.
pay (of soldiers), stipendium.
pay honour, honorem habere.
peace, pax.
peacefully, tranquille.
peck, modius.
Pelopidas, -dae.
pen, calamus.
penalty, poena.
people, populus.
perceive, cerno, sentio, video, animadverto, intelligo.
perform, ago, perficio.
perform a promise, praesto.
perhaps, fortassis, fortasse.
peril, periculum, discrimen.
perish, pereo, intereo.
permission, facultas.
permit, sino.
persevere, persevero.
person (bodily form), corpus.
person (in), coram.
person (human being), persona.
pervade, compleo, imbuo.
petitioner, interpellans.
Philip, Philippus.
philosopher, philosophus.
philosophy, philosophia.
physician, medicus.
pick out, deligo.
pick up, excipio.
picked, delectus.
picture, tabula.
pierce, transfigo.
pierce through, transverbero.
pilot, gubernator.
pin (not a) to choose, nihil interest.
pioneer, munitor.
pipe, tibia.

piper, tibicen.
Piso, -onis.
pit, fovea.
place, locus.
place, (vb.), pono, colloco.
place a garrison, loco.
plague, pestis.
plain, campus.
  in the plain, in plano.
plan, (vb.), molior, cogito, constituo.
plan (design), consilium.
plane (tree), platanus.
planet, errans sidus.
plant, vb. (a tree), sero.
plant (a standard), statuo.
plant (a dart), figo.
plate (silver), argentum.
Plato, -onis.
play (drama), fabula.
play (vb.), ludo.
play (on an instrument), cano.
pleasant, iucundus.
please, placeo (dat.).
pleasing, gratus.
pleasure, voluptas.
pleasure-grounds, horti.
pledge, pignus.
  to pledge one's word, do fidem.
plough, aratrum.
plough (vb.), aro.
pluck, carpo.
plunder, praeda.
plunder (vb.), expilo.
plunge headlong, praecipitare se.
poem, carmen.
poet, poeta.
point (to be just on the) of, in eo esse ut. . . .
point to, monstro.
poison, venenum.
poison (vb.), veneno neco.
Polemo, -monis.
policy, consilium.
polish thoroughly, perpolio.
Pompeians, Pompeiani.
pontiff, pontifex.
poor, pauper.
poplar, populus.
populace, multitudo.

portrait, imago.
position, status, res, condicio.
position (*of an army*), castra.
position (*of a place*), locus or loca (*pl.*).
possess, obtineo, possideo.
possession (*to get*), potior.
possession (*to take*), occupo.
possession (*to be in*), obtineo, possideo.
post (*a letter*), do.
post troops, oppono, loco.
posterity, posteri.
postpone, postpono.
potent, prodigium.
poverty, paupertas, egestas.
power, potestas, potentia.
powerful, validus, potens.
practice, exercitatio.
practice (*to have*), exercere artem.
practice (*custom*), consuetudo.
praetor, praetor.
praise, laus.
praise (*vb.*), laudo.
praiseworthy, laudabilis.
pray, precor.
precaution (*to take*), caveo.
precedent, exemplum.
precept, praeceptum.
precise, accuratus.
precisely, prorsus.
predict, praedico.
pre-eminent, (*to be*), emineo.
prefer, praefero, praepono, antepono.
   in preference to all others, potissimum.
prepare, paro.
prepare for, comparo.
present (*being*), praesens.
present (*vb.*), dono, do.
present (*exhibit*), praebeo.
present difficulties, ea quae nunc premunt.
   at the present day, hodie.
preservation, salus.
preserve, servo, conservo, retineo.
preside, praesideo.
press forward, procedo.
press on, contendo.

pretence, simulatio.
prevail, valeo.
prevent, obsto, impedio, prohibeo.
Priam, Priamus.
price, pretium.
pride, arrogantia, superbia.
priest, sacerdos.
priesthood, sacerdotium.
prison, carcer.
prisoner, captivus, deditus.
private, privatus.
privately, privatim.
probably, fortasse.
proceed, pergo, proficiscor.
proceed with, ago.
procession, pompa.
proclaim, pronuntio.
prodigy, monstrum.
produce (*vb.*), effero, profero, produco.
produce (*give birth to*), gigno.
produce an effect, efficio.
productive, fertilis, fecundus.
productiveness, fecunditas.
profess, profiteor.
proffer, offero.
profit, lucrum, fructus.
profitable (*to be*), prosum.
profligacy, nequitia.
progress, progressus.
project, consilium.
prolong, profero.
promise (*vb.*), spondeo, polliceor.
promise, fides.
proof, specimen.
prop up, fulcio.
properly, recte.
property, bona (*pl.*), res.
prophet, vates.
propose, pronuntio, propono.
prosecute, voco in iudicium.
Proserpine, Proserpina.
prosperity, res prosperae, res secundae.
prosperous, fortunatus.
protect, defendo, munio, arceo, tego.
protected (*covered*), tectus.
protection, praesidium.
prove, probo.

prove (*turn out*), exsto.
provide, instruo.
province, provincia.
provoke, lacesso.
public, publicus.
public affairs, res publica.
public office, honos.
public speaker, orator.
publicly, palam, publice.
    matters of public interest, quae ad publicum pertinent.
publish, edo.
pull out, evello.
pumps (*work at*), sentinam exhaurire.
punishment, supplicium, poena.
purchase, emo.
purpose (*set*), institutum.
    to no purpose, frustra, nequicquam.
purposely, ex industria.
pursuit, studium.
push away, submoveo.
put, pono.
put an end to, conficio.
put aside, repono.
put down, opprimo, *perf.* oppressi.
put forward, profero.
put in chains, vincio.
put in danger, facio periculum (*dat.*).
put in prison, dare in custodiam.
put on trial, facere reum.
put out (*eyes*), privo.
put to death, neco.
put to the sword, trucido.

Qualities (*good*), virtutes.
quantity, vis.
quarrel, inimicitia.
queen, regina.
quench, sedo.
question, quaestio.
    I do not question, non dubito quin.
quick, celer.
quickly, celeriter.
quite, admodum.
quite (*by far*), longe.

Rack (*vb.*), vexo.
raft, ratis.
rains (*it*), pluit.
raise hopes, adduco in spem.
rally, colligo.
ram, aries.
rampart, vallum.
rank, nobilitas, dignitas.
ransom (*vb.*), redimo.
ratified, ratus.
rattle (*vb.*), crepo.
reach, venio ad, adipiscor.
reach (*in safety*), pervenio.
reach (*after a voyage*), teneo.
read, lego.
readily, libenter.
readiness, facultas.
ready, paratus.
    get ready (*prepare*), paro.
realised (*to be*), evenio.
rear (*in the*), post tergum.
reason, causa, ratio.
    not without reason, non immerito.
    for that reason, eo.
rebuild, restituo.
recall, domum revoco.
receive, recipio, -cepi, accipio.
recklessly, temere.
recklessness, temeritas.
reckon, habeo.
recognise, cognosco.
reconciled (*to be*), in gratiam redire.
reconnoitre, speculor.
recover (*from a swoon*), despicio.
rectitude, honestas.
refreshment, cibus.
refuse, nego, abnuo.
regard (*vb.*), duco, accipio.
regard with favour, faveo.
    to be regarded with affection, carus haberi.
    to have a high regard for, diligo.
regular, constans.
regulate, rego.
reign, regnum.
reign (*vb.*), regno.
reinforcements, supplementum.
rejected (*to be*), repulsam ferre.
relation, cognatus.
release (*vb.*), dimitto.

relief, auxilium.
relieve, libero, auxilior.
relieve (diminish), levo.
religion, religio.
religious-scruples, religio.
relinquish, cedo.
rely on, sto.
remain, maneo, remaneo.
remaining (adj.), reliquus.
remark, verbum.
remarkable, singularis, insignis.
remember, memini, mihi venit in mentem.
remembrance, memoria.
remind, admoneo.
reminiscence, memoria.
remnant, reliquiae.
remote part, secretum.
remove, tollo.
rend, carpo.
render, ago.
renown, gloria.
repair, reficio.
repeatedly, iterum atque iterum.
repent, poeniteo.
reply, responsum.
reply (to letter), (vb.), rescribo.
reply (send a), rescribo.
report, rumor, fama.
report (vb.), renuntio.
represent, induco, expono, fingo, facio.
represent (as a work of art), exprimo.
repulse (vb.), repello.
reputation, fama.
repute (to be in bad) with, in odio esse apud.
repute (to have a bad), male audire.
request (vb.), rogo, peto.
require, postulo.
require (need), requiro.
require to do something, impero.
rescue (vb.), eripio.
resemblance, similitudo.
resentment, dolor, ira.
reserve (without), aperte.
resignation (with), patienter.
resist, resto.
resound, sono.

resources, opes.
respect (vb.), colo, vereor.
rest, quies.
rest (vb.), acquiesco.
rest (the), ceteri.
rest of, reliquus.
rest on, fultum esse.
restore, restituo.
restrain, arceo.
result, eventus.
retain one's senses, esse sanae mentis.
retake, recipio.
retire, se recipere, gradum referre.
retirement, solitudo.
retiring, modestus.
retreat, receptus.
return, reditus.
return (vb.), reverto, redeo, recipere se.
revel, gaudeo.
revenge, ultio.
revenge (vb.), ulciscor.
reverential feeling, religio.
reverse, mutatio.
review (vb.), lustro.
reward, proemium.
   with a reward, donatus.
Rhegium, Rhegium.
Rhine, Rhenus.
Rhodes, Rhodus.
rich, dives.
rich (district), opimus.
riches, divitiae.
ridge (of hill), iugum.
ridiculous, ridiculus.
right (in morals), honestum.
right (on the), dexter.
right-hand, dextra.
rightly, iure, recte.
ring, anulus.
rise, surgo.
risk, periculum.
rival (vb.), aequo.
river, flumen, amnis.
road, iter, via.
rob, spolio.
robber, latro, praedo.
robber of temples, sacrilegus.
roll (vb.), voluto.
roof, tectum.

room, cubiculum.
room (*place*), locus.
rose, rosa.
roughness of manner, animi ferocitas.
rout, fundo.
ruin, pernicies, exitium.
ruined (*to be*), concido, pereo.
rule (*vb.*), guberno, imperito (*dat.*).
rule, regula, norma.
  under one's rule, subiectus.
run, curro.
run a risk, adire periculum, committere se discrimini.
run away, fugio.
run to and fro, curso.
runaway, fugitivus.
rush, ruo, curro.
rush into, incurro.
rush out, eicere se.

Sabine, Sabinus.
sacred, sacer.
sacrifice, sacrificium.
sacrifice (*give up*), iacturam facio.
sacrifice (*offer as a*), immolo.
sacrifice one's life, caput voveo.
safe, tutus, salvus, incolumis.
safely, tuto.
safety, salus.
sage, prudens, sapiens.
sage conduct, quae recte fiunt.
Saguntines, Saguntini.
sail (*vb.*), navigo.
sailor, nauta.
sally forth, erumpo, exeo.
salute (*vb.*), saluto.
same, idem.
Samnites, -itium.
sanctity (*of an oath*), fides.
Sarpedon, -onis.
satisfy, satis facio (*dat.*).
satisfy (*convince*), persuadeo (*dat.*).
Saturn, Saturnus.
savage, crudelis, immanis.
save, servo, subvenio (*dat.*).
say, dico, aio, inquam.
say no more about, omitto.
  to say nothing of, praeter.
  to say nothing, tacere.

scale, ascendo, evado in.
scanty (*very*), perpaucus.
scarcely, vix.
scarcity, inopia.
science, ars, scientia.
Scipio, -onis.
sea, mare.
sea (*adj.*), maritimus.
sea-fight, pugna navalis.
search after, quaero.
seat, sedes, sella.
  take a seat, consido.
secretly, clam (*adv.*).
security (*in*), tuto.
see, video, sentio, conspicio.
see before others, praevideo.
see clearly, perspicio.
see (*visit*), viso.
seek, peto, quaero.
seek again (*reseek*), repeto.
seek eagerly, appeto.
seem, videor.
seize, capio, rapio.
seldom, raro.
select, deligo.
self-indulgence, luxuria.
sell, vendo.
  to be sold, veneo.
seller, venditor.
Senate, Senatus.
senate-house, curia.
senator, senator.
senatorial, senatorius.
send, mitto.
send back, remitto.
send forward, praemitto.
sensation, sensus.
senses (*to retain one's*), sanae mentis esse.
sensible, prudens.
sentiment, sententia.
separate (*vb.*), separo.
serious, gravis.
serve (*to be inclined to*), inservio.
service, officium.
  to be serviceable, esse usui.
servility, obsequium.
set (*as the sun*), occido.
set foot, ingredior.
set up, statuo.

set (*an example*), praebeo.
set at *nought*, negligo, contemno,
set *out*, proficiscor.
settle (*as a mist*), sedeo.
severity (*as of cold*), vis.
severity *of a master*, saevitia.
shade, umbra.
shake, quatio.
shameful, infamis.
share (*vb.*), partior.
sharp, acutus.
sharpen, acuo.
shave, tondeo.
sheep, ovis, pecus, -udis.
shelter (*under*), in tectis.
she-wolf, lupa.
shield, scutum, clipeus.
shift (*vb.*), transfero, confero.
ship, navis.
shoot, mitto.
shop, taberna.
shore, ora, litus.
short, brevis, exiguus.
shoulder, umerus.
shout, clamor.
shout (*vb.*), conclamo.
show, monstro, praebeo.
shrine, fanum.
shrink *from*, fugio, defugio.
shun, discedo a.
shut *up*, claudo.
Sicilians, Siculus.
Sicily, Sicilia.
sick, aeger, aegrotus.
sickness, aegritudo.
side, latus.
    on *both sides*, utrimque.
    on *all sides*, undique.
siege, oppugnatio, obsidio.
siege *works*, opera (*pl.*).
    to *commence a siege*, obsideo.
sight, adspectus, conspectus.
    in *the sight of*, in conspectu, in
        oculis.
sign, signum.
signal, signum.
silence, silentium.
silent, tacitus.
silver, argentum.
silver (*adj.*), argenteus.

sin, turpia (*pl.*).
sing, cano.
single, unicus.
sink, sido.
sister, soror.
sit, sedeo.
situation, locus.
skilful, peritus, sciens.
skill *in archery*, ars sagittandi.
sky, caelum.
slain, caesus.
slaughter, caedes, strages.
slaughter (*vb.*), immolo, trucido.
slave, servus.
slavery, servitus.
    to *be in slavery*, servio.
slay, occido, interficio, caedo, in-
    terimo, trucido.
sleep, somnus.
sleep (*vb.*), dormio.
slight, parvus.
sloth, inertia, desidia.
slow, tardus.
small, parvus, exiguus.
smile, risus.
smile (*vb.*), rideo.
smoke, fumus.
snake, anguis.
snatch, rapio.
snow, nix.
so, sic, ita; tam.
so *far from* . . . *but even*, non
    modo non . . . sed etiam.
so (*to such an extent*), adeo.
so *much as*, aeque quam, tam—quam.
sober *earnestness* (*in*), vero et serio.
soberness (*with*), bona fruge.
soldier, miles.
solicit, peto.
solitude, solitudo.
son, filius, natus.
song, cantus.
sorest *need* (*time of*), maxime ne-
    cessarium.
soothe, lenio.
soothsayer, haruspex.
sorrow, dolor, maeror, tristitia.
soul (*mind*), animus.
soul (*spirit*), anima, animus.
sound, sonitus, vox.

sound (vb.), sono.
sound knowledge (to have), prudenter intelligo.
  to sound a signal for retreat, signum receptui canere.
source, fons.
south-wind, auster.
sovereignty, imperium,
sow, sero.
space, spatium.
Spain, Hispania.
Spaniards, Hispani.
spare, parco (dat.).
Spartans, Lacedaemonii,
speak, dico, loquor.
speak well, eloquens esse.
speak highly of, laudo.
  speaker (a fine), orator.
spear, hasta.
spectator (to be a), specto.
spectator, spectator.
speech, oratio.
speech (a set), oratio.
speed, cursus.
spend (pass), ago.
spendthrift, prodigus.
spirit, animus.
spirit (dash), spiritus.
splendid, insignis, clarus.
spontaneously, sponte sua, ultro.
spot (place), locus.
spread, spargo.
spring (season), ver.
spring (of water), fons.
spring from (a source), fluo ex.
spy (vb.), speculor.
squadron, turma.
squadron of ships, naves.
squander, effundo.
stake, sudes.
  is at stake, agitur.
stand, sto.
stand before, adsto (dat.).
standard, signum.
standard of measurement, regula, norma.
star, stella, sidus.
state (vb.), (explain), demonstro.
state (assert), dico.
state (country), res publica, civitas.

station, locus.
station (vb.), loco.
statue, signum, statua.
stature, statura.
statute, lex.
stay, maneo.
  to stay with Caesar, apud Caesarem esse.
steep, arduus.
steer (a course), teneo.
steer (a ship), dirigo.
steer (for a place), peto.
step, gradus, passus.
  to take a step (in walking), gradum facere.
step by step, ordine.
stepmother, noverca.
stern, puppis.
stillness, silentium.
stir, tumultus.
stir a step, pedem efferre.
Stoics, Stoici.
stone, lapis.
stone (vb.), lapides iacio.
stone (adj.), lapideus.
stop (vb.), prohibeo.
stop on (loiter), commoror.
stores, res.
storm, tempestas.
storm (vb.), oppugno.
story, fabula.
stoutly, fortiter, acri animo.
straight, rectus.
straightforward, rectus.
straightway, continuo.
strait (between continents), divortium.
strange, mirus.
strategy, consilium.
stream, rivus.
street, platea.
strength, robur, vis.
strengthen (a fort), munio.
strike down (slay), interficio.
striking (likeness), maximus.
strip, nudo.
strive, contendo.
strong, firmus.
  very strong support, summa studia.

struck with admiration, admiratus.
struggle, dimicatio.
  have a struggle, contendo.
study, studium.
stupid, hebes.
style, genus.
style (*vb.*), dico.
surrender, deditio.
surrender (*vb.*), dedo, prodo.
surround, cingo, circumvenio.
suspicion, suspicio.
subdue, subigo, -egi, domo.
subject, res.
subject-matter, res.
submit, patior.
subsequently, postea.
subservient (*to be*), servio.
subterranean, sub terra.
succeed, impetro.
success, victoria.
successful, felix.
succession (*in*), deinceps, in orbem.
sudden, subitus.
sudden (*on a*), repente, subito.
suddenly, subito.
suffer, patior.
suffer (*pay a penalty*), do poenas.
suffer (*from disease*), afficior.
suffering (*adj.*), laborans.
sufferings, poenae.
sufficient for, tantum . . . ut
  satis. . . .
sufficiently, satis.
suit (*vb.*), congruo (*dat.*).
suitable, aptus, idoneus.
summer, aestas.
summer (*adj.*), aestivus.
summon, adhibeo.
sun, sol.
  at sunrise, sole orto, prima luce.
  at sunset, solis occasu.
sunshine, sol.
superabundance, multitudo.
superfluous, supervacaneus.
superior, praestantior.
superior (*to be*), supero.
superstition, superstitio.
suppliant, supplex.
supply (*vb.*), praebeo.
supply of corn, res frumentaria.

suppose, existimor, reor.
supreme influence (*to have*), plurimum posse.
sure, certus.
sure (*to be*), pro certo habeo, confido, exploratum habeo.
surely, vero.
surface of, summus.
surpass, supero.
surprise (*vb.*), opprimo.
sway, ditio.
sweet, dulcis.
swell (*vb.*), cresco.
swim, nato, no.
sword, gladius, ferrum.
Syracusans, Syracusani.
Syracuse, Syracusae.

Table, mensa.
taint, contagio.
take, sumo.
take (*a town*), capio, armis capio.
take (*lead*), duco.
take across, traduco.
take an oath, iuror or iuro.
take away, aufero, adimo, detraho,
  abduco.
take care, provideo.
take care of, indulgeo.
take heed, video.
take in hand, suscipio.
take out, effero.
take pains, operam do.
take possession, occupo, obtineo.
take thought for, habeo procura-
  tionem, prospicio.
take up, sumo, capio, fero, suscipio.
taken prisoner, captus.
talent (*of silver*), talentum.
talents, ingenium.
talk (*vb.*), loquor, fabulor.
tall, altus.
tax, vectigal.
teach, doceo.
teacher, magister.
tear away, avello.
tell, narro, dico.
temper, animus.
temple, aedes, templum.
Terence, Terentius.

terribly (*severely*), graviter.
terrify, terreo.
territory, fines (*pl.*).
test (*vb.*), metior.
testy, amarus.
Thames, Tamesis.
thank, gratias ago.
theatre, theatrum.
Thebes, Thebae (*pl.*).
there, ibi, eo.
therefore, igitur, itaque.
therefore (emphatic), proinde.
thereupon, inde.
Thermopylae, Thermopylae (*pl.*).
Thessaly, Thessalia.
thick, densus.
think, sentio, puto, existimo, arbitror.
think of, cogito de.
thirst, sitis.
thorough insight (*to have a*), perspectum habeo.
thought, mens, cogitatio.
threaten (*as a danger*), impendo, impendeo.
threaten (*as a fort*), immineo.
threats, minae.
three years, *space of*, triennium.
throb, mico.
thronged with visitors (*to be*), celebrari.
throw, iacio.
throw away, abicio.
throw down, deicio.
throw over (*as a garment*), inicio.
thunderbolt, fulmen.
Tiber, -eris.
till, colo.
tillage, agricultura.
time, tempus, aetas.
   at a later time, ad posterum.
   for a long time, diu.
   for a short time, paulisper.
   once on a time, aliquando.
   after a time, ex intervallo.
   for the first time, primum.
time-honoured, vetustissimus.
timorous, timidus.
Tiresias, ae.
title (*get a*), appellor.

to-day, hodie.
together, una.
toil, labor.
toilsome, laboriosus.
tomb, tumulus, sepulcrum.
to-morrow, cras.
tongue, lingua.
too (*also*), quoque, etiam.
too much, nimium, nimis.
tooth, dens.
top, cacumen.
topic, locus.
torture, cruciatus.
totter, labo.
touch, tango.
touch of madness, furor.
touch upon, attingo.
tower, turris.
town, oppidum.
   out of town, extra urbem.
trader, mercator.
traduce, maledico.
tragedy, tragoedia.
transform, converto.
translate, transfero.
transmit, trado.
transported with joy (*to be*), efferor.
traverse, peragro.
tread down, obtero.
treasure (*royal*), gaza.
treasury (*public*), aerarium.
treat, ago, tracto.
treatise, liber.
treaty, foedus.
tree, arbor.
trench, fossa.
trial, iudicium.
   on trial, reus.
tribunal, tribunal.
tribune, tribunus.
tribune in the army, tribunus militum.
tribuneship, tribunatus.
tribunicial, tribunicius.
trifler, nugator.
triumph, triumphus.
Trojan, Troianus.
troop (*of women*), grex.
troops, copiae, milites.
trouble, cura, dolor, sollicitudo.

troubles, miseriae, mala (*pl.*).
Troy, Troia.
truce, indutiae.
true, verus.
true (perfect), solidus.
trumpet, tuba.
trunk (of elephant), manus.
trust (vb.), credo (*dat.*).
   I trust I may . . ., utinam *with subj.*
trusty, fidelis.
truth, veritas.
try, conor, tempto *or* tento.
try to get, peto.
try to persuade not to do . . ., dehortor ne . .
tuition, institutio.
turn, verto.
turn away (the eyes), deflecto.
turn out well, prospere cedere.
turn out (become), evado.
turn upside down, inverto.
two days (space of), biduum.
two years (space of), biennium.
tyrant, tyrannus.

Umpire, arbiter.
unarmed, inermis.
unbounded, summus.
uncertain, incertus.
uncle (maternal), avunculus.
uncle (paternal), patruus.
under, sub.
under control, domitus.
understand, intelligo.
   I do not understand, nescio.
undertake, suscipio, sumo.
undertake (promise to do), polliceor.
undeservedly, immerito.
undeserving, indignus.
undone (to be), pereo.
unexpected, improvisus.
unexpectedly, de improviso.
unfair, iniustus.
unfavourable, iniquus.
ungodly, impius.
ungrounded, falsus.
unhallowed, inauspicatus.
uninformed, ignarus.
universe, mundus.

unknown to fame, ignobilis.
unlucky, infelix.
unpopular (to be), in odio esse.
unprepared, imparatus.
unsafe, lubricus.
unwary, incautus.
unwilling, invitus.
unworthy, indignus.
up to, tenus.
uphold, sustineo.
uplift, effero, suffero.
upright, iustus.
upset, everto.
use (vb.), utor.
   with your usual courtesy, qua soles comitate.
   to use the phrase of Cicero, ut ait Cicero.
usurp, invado.
utter (a word), mitto.
utterly, funditus.

Valley, valles *or* vallis.
valour, virtus.
value (vb.), aestimo.
van, prima acies.
vanquish, vinco.
vanquished (utterly), devictus.
Varro, -onis.
vast, ingens, numerosus.
vast number, multitudo.
vastly, magnopere *or* magno opere.
vein, vena.
venture (vb.), audeo.
Venus, -eris.
verse, versus.
vessel, vas.
veteran (adj.), veteranus.
vexation, molestia.
vexed (to be), aegre fero.
vice, vitium.
victorious, victor, victrix.
victory, victoria.
views, sententia.
vigour, vis.
vine, vitis.
violate, polluo.
violation of (in), adversus (*prep.*).
violence, vis.

virtue, virtus.
virtuous, probus.
visit (vb.), viso, venio ad.
voice, vox.
   with one voice, uno ore.
Volscians, Volsci.
volume, magnitudo.
vote (in senate), decerno.
vow (vb.), voveo.
voyage, navigatio.
vulture, vultur.

Wage, gero.
wage (war) on, infero.
wait, maneo.
wait for, maneo.
waiting-maid, ancilla.
walk (vb.), ambulo, ingredior.
walk (of animals), gradior, ingredior.
wall, murus.
want (ask for), peto.
want (be without), egeo, careo.
want of control, licentia.
wanting (to be), desum.
war, bellum.
war (vb.), gero bellum.
warlike look (to have a), spectare
   ad castra.
ward off, propulso.
warn, calidus.
warmth (of affection), vis.
warn, moneo, admoneo.
warning, monitum, admonitio, signum.
wary, cautus.
wash, lavo.
waste (vb.), consumo, sumpsi.
watch, servo.
watchfulness, diligentia.
water, aqua.
wax great, cresco.
way, via, iter.
weak, infirmus, imbecillis.
weaken, infirmo.
wealth, divitiae, opes.
wealthy, opulens.
weapon, telum.
weapons (pl.), arma.

wear the appearance of, spectare
   ad.
weary, fessus.
weary (vb.), fatigo.
weep, fleo.
weeping, fletus.
weigh, expendo.
weigh anchor, solvere naves.
weight, pondus.
weighty, gravis, magnus.
welfare, salus.
well, puteus.
well (adv.), bene.
well (to be), valeo.
well (to be not very), minus valeo.
well aware, non nescius.
well known, clarus.
   it is well known, constat.
west, occidens.
whence, unde.
where, ubi, qua.
whereas, autem.
whisper in ear, insusurro.
whit (not a), nihilo.
white, albus, candidus.
whithersoever, qua.
whole, totus, cunctus.
wholesome, saluber.
   one's whole life, omne tempus
     aetatis.
why, cur, quare, quam ob rem,
   quid?
why do you not . . . ? quin . . . ?
wicked, scelestus, sceleratus.
wickedness, scelus.
wicked thing, peccatum.
wide, latus.
wide (adv.), late.
width, latitudo.
wife, coniunx, uxor.
wild beast, fera.
wild olive-tree, oleaster.
will (testament), testamentum.
will (desire), voluntas.
willing, libens, lubens.
willingly, libenter, lubenter.
win (lands), possideo.
win (a camp), potior.
wind, ventus.
window, fenestra.

wine, vinum.
wing (of army), cornu.
wing (of bird), ala.
wing (of insect), penna.
winter, bruma, hiemps.
winter-quarters, hiberna.
wisdom, sapientia.
wise, sapiens,
wise (worldly), prudens.
wise (to be), sapio.
wisely, sapienter.
wish (vb.), opto, volo.
wish (desire), voluntas.
with this restriction, ita . . . ut. .
withdraw (go away), excedo, cedo, recipere se.
withdraw (take away), subduco, abstraho.
without (to be), careo.
witness, testis.
wittily, urbane.
wolf, lupus, lupa.
woman, femina, mulier.
wonderful, mirificus, mirus.
wont (to be), soleo.
wood, silva.
wool, lana.
woollen, laneus.
word, verbum.
word (promise), fides.
work, opus, opera, labor.
workshop, officina.
worse, deterior, peior.
worship (vb.), colo.
worth, virtus.

worthless, nequam, perditus.
worthless (book), malus.
wound, vulnus.
wound (vb.), vulnero.
wounded, saucius.
wrath, ira.
wrathfulness, iracundia.
wreath, corona.
wretched, miser.
write, scribo,
writing, scriptum.
writing (act of), scriptio.
wrong (vb.), violo.
wrong (to do), pecco.
wrong (act of), iniuria.
wrong (dishonest), turpis.

Xenophon, -ontis.

Years *(space of two)*, biennium.
years (three), triennium.
years (four,) quadriennium.
yellow, flavus.
yesterday, heri.
yield, cedo, decedo.
yoke, iugum.
you will have it so, ita vis.
young, iuvenis.
young man, adulescens.
young (offspring), proles.
your (sing.), tuus.
your (pl.), vester.
youth (time of life), adulescentia.

𝕰𝖉𝖎𝖓𝖇𝖚𝖗𝖌𝖍 𝖀𝖓𝖎𝖛𝖊𝖗𝖘𝖎𝖙𝖞 𝕻𝖗𝖊𝖘𝖘:

THOMAS AND ARCHIBALD CONSTABLE, PRINTERS TO HER MAJESTY.

www.ingramcontent.com/pod-product-compliance
Lightning Source LLC
Chambersburg PA
CBHW022351020726

47500CB00002B/228